The Espionage and Sedition Acts

The Espionage and Sedition Acts of 1917–1918 mark one of the most controversial moments in American history. Even as President Woodrow Wilson justified U.S. entry into World War I on the grounds that it would "make the world safe for democracy," the act curtailed civil liberties at home by making it illegal to speak out against the U.S. participation in the conflict. Supporters of the Acts argued that these measures were necessary to protect national security and keep in check the perceived threat of radical activities, while opponents considered them an unjustifiable breach of the Bill of Rights. The conflict between government powers and civil liberties concretized by the Acts continues to resonate today.

The Espionage and Sedition Acts introduces students to this controversial set of laws, the cultural and political context in which they were passed, and their historical ramifications. In a concise narrative supplemented by primary sources including court cases, newspaper articles, and personal papers, Mitchell Newton-Matza gives students of history and politics a nuanced understanding of this key event.

Mitchell Newton-Matza has taught at numerous colleges in Illinois, Virginia and Colorado. He is the author of *Intelligent and Honest Radicals: The Chicago Federation and the Politics of Progression* (2013).

Critical Moments in American History

Edited by William Thomas Allison, Georgia Southern University

The Emergence of Rock and Roll
Music and the Rise of American Youth Culture
Mitchell K. Hall

Transforming Civil War Prisons
Lincoln, Lieber, and the Politics of Captivity
Paul J. Springer and Glenn Robins

The Battle of Fort Sumter
The First Shots of the American Civil War
Wesley Moody

The WPA
Creating Jobs and Hope in the Great Depression
Sandra Opdycke

The California Gold Rush
The Stampede that Changed the World
Mark Eifler

Bleeding Kansas
Slavery, Sectionalism, and Civil War on the Missouri-Kansas Border
Michael E. Woods

The Marshall Plan
A New Deal for Europe
Michael Holm

The Espionage and Sedition Acts
World War I and the Image of Civil Liberties
Mitchell Newton-Matza

The Espionage and Sedition Acts

World War I and the Image of Civil Liberties

Mitchell Newton-Matza

Routledge
Taylor & Francis Group

NEW YORK AND LONDON

First published 2017
by Routledge
711 Third Avenue, New York, NY 10017

and by Routledge
2 Park Square, Milton Park, Abingdon, Oxon, OX14 4RN

Routledge is an imprint of the Taylor & Francis Group, an informa business

© 2017 Taylor & Francis

British Library Cataloguing in Publication Data
A catalogue record for this book is available from the British Library

Library of Congress Cataloging in Publication Data
A catalog record for this book has been requested

ISBN: 978-1-138-02303-1
ISBN: 978-1-138-02304-8
ISBN: 978-1-315-77671-2

Typeset in Bembo
by Integra Software Service Pvt. Ltd.

This book is dedicated to the loving memory of my father, Charles A. Matza. Dad, you instilled a love of history, and learning in general. Now that you are back with Mom, I am sure you are still talking about the time you had your head under the car hood and I accidentally honked the horn right into your ear.

Contents

Series Introduction

Welcome to the Routledge *Critical Moments in American History* series. The purpose of this new series is to give students a window into the historian's craft through concise, readable books by leading scholars, who bring together the best scholarship and engaging primary sources to explore a critical moment in the American past. In discovering the principal points of the story in these books, gaining a sense of historiography, following a fresh trail of primary documents, and exploring suggested readings, students can then set out on their own journey, to debate the ideas presented, interpret primary sources, and reach their own conclusions—just like the historian.

A critical moment in history can be a range of things—a pivotal year, the pinnacle of a movement or trend, or an important event such as the passage of a piece of legislation, an election, a court decision, a battle. It can be social, cultural, political, or economic. It can be heroic or tragic. Whatever they are, such moments are by definition "game changers," momentous changes in the pattern of the American fabric, paradigm shifts in the American experience. Many of the critical moments explored in this series are familiar; some less so.

There is no ultimate list of critical moments in American history—any group of students, historians, or other scholars may come up with a different catalog of topics. These differences of view, however, are what make history itself and the study of history so important and so fascinating. Therein can be found the utility of historical inquiry—to explore, to challenge, to understand, and to realize the legacy of the past through its influence of the present. It is the hope of this series to help students realize this intrinsic value of our past and of studying our past.

William Thomas Allison
Georgia Southern University

Acknowledgments

I thought about doing this book for a very long time. When I saw Routledge was looking for specific manuscripts, I took the time to work up a proposal, much of which was written on plane rides between Virginia and Colorado. When I finally settled in the Denver area, I was able to perfect—with critiques from the publisher's readers—the proposal. When I started working on the manuscript, the Jefferson County, Colorado, and Denver Public Libraries had numerous source materials that assisted me. In addition, the trial of *The Masses*, as seen in Chapter 3, came from a paper I wrote while in my doctoral program, as did the section on the Industrial Workers of the World in Chapter 5.

To those who assisted me along the way, I heartily thank you. First, I thank Genevieve Aoki and Daniel Finaldi at Routledge for their help and patience. I also thank my comrades from the Denver Art Museum for their moral support and interest in this project. I must mention first my former comrades from the Guest Services department where I started. Molly Delandsheer, Kevin Rollins, Katie Bukowski, Lis Link, Valarie Castillo, and Jeff King (who hired me in the first place) have especially made my time at the DAM fun and rewarding. I must also thank the entire Protective Services team, who I joined after the Guest Services temporary position ended, for their friendship and encouragement.

Other people in my life who were there for me include my family, Carlos Cortes, my Chicago attorney Maggie Aguilar, Freddy Atkins, Jason Lewis, Robert Moore, Michelle Lynn, David Southwell, Nancy Hendricks, Robyn Webb, and Carmen Gomez-Galisteo. And, as usual, I must thank Karen Brad, Kelly Carevic, Chere LaRose, Ari Peach, Hala Abdulla and Basema Maki. My fiancée Josie Brissette has never let me down no matter how bad things might get. Last, and certainly not least, is my 18-year-old daughter Safira, who remains the light of my life and is wise beyond her years. Her acceptance into the University of Massachusetts only confirmed how bright she is, and I still rely on her for advice.

About the Author

Mitchell Newton-Matza received his PhD in history from The Catholic University of America in Washington, DC. He has taught at several colleges in the Chicago and Washington DC areas. He is the editor and chief contributor to the book *Jazz Age: People and Perspectives*, (ABC-CLIO, 2009), a work that has received excellent reviews. He contributed two chapters to the Railroads volume in the 9-volume series *The Industrial Revolution in America* (ABC-CLIO, 2005). His latest works are *Intelligent and Honest Radicals: The Chicago Federation of Labor and the Politics of Progression* (Lexington Books) and as editor/contributor of *Disasters and Tragic Events: An Encyclopedia of Catastrophes in American History* (ABC-CLIO), which were both released in 2014. His other latest work, *An Encyclopedia of Historic Sites and Landmarks* (ABC-CLIO) is scheduled for release in the fall of 2016. In addition to his books and book chapters he is also the author of over 35 reference and encyclopedia pieces. In addition, his fiction work, *The Transitioning: An Emotional Journey for the Nomadic Mind* was published in 2015 through Xlibris. He currently resides in Denver, Colorado.

Timeline

1914

June 28   Austrian Arch-Duke and heir to the Habsburg throne Franz Ferdinand is assassinated along with his wife, Sophie, in Sarajevo, Bosnia.

July 5   Germany issues the infamous *blank cheque* to Austria-Hungary, promising its support in whatever decision the latter makes.

July 23   Austria-Hungary issues an ultimatum to Serbia as evidence mounts that officials in the Serbian government either knew about the assassination plans, or participated.

July 25   Serbia rejects part of the ultimatum on the basis of national sovereignty; diplomatic relations are broken off.

July 28   Austria-Hungary declares war on Serbia.

July 29   Austria-Hungary refuses to negotiate with Serbia. Russia orders military mobilization against Austria-Hungary to begin July 31, with France also pledging to back up this action.

August 3   Germany declares war on France over its neutrality ultimatum; Great Britain begins its mobilization.

August 4   Great Britain declares war on Germany after the Germans invade Belgium. U.S. President Woodrow Wilson officially proclaims American neutrality.

August 6   Austria declares war against Russia. Great Britain issues a statement justifying its blockade of Germany over American protests concerning neutrality.

August 12   Great Britain and France declare war on Austria.

1915

February 4   Germany declares the British Isles a war zone effective February 15.

February 10   The U.S. protests the German declaration as another violation of their neutrality. The Germans warned the American government that further actions would be at their own risk, with the use of submarines to enforce this blockade.

April 11   Germany presses upon Americans to stop selling arms to the Allies.

May 7	Despite German warnings to Americans, a German submarine sank the British ocean liner Lusitania. Some 128 Americans lost their lives, with a total death count of 1,198.
May 13–July 21	A series of statements known as the *Lusitania Notes* condemned the German use of unrestricted submarine warfare.

1916

June 3	The National Defense Act is passed in increasing the size of the military.
July 30	Fears of German sabotage on American soil increases as a munitions plant on Black Tom Island, New Jersey, explodes.
August 31	Germany exceeds to international wishes and declared it will cease submarine warfare.
November 17	Utilizing his slogan of "He Kept Us Out of War," Wilson is re-elected president.

1917

January 16	Arthur Zimmerman, the German foreign minister, sends a coded telegram to Mexico proposing entering the war on their side. The Germans promised, among other items, restoration of former Mexican territory lost to the U.S. during the previous century.
January 31–February 3	Germany abandons its previous pledge and resumes unrestricted submarine warfare. The U.S. severs all diplomatic ties with Germany.
March 1	The contents of the Zimmerman Telegram are revealed. Wilson subsequently asks Congress for the authority to arm American merchantmen.
March 15	The first revolution of the year occurs in Russia, deposing Tsar Nicholas II and his family.
April 2	Wilson, in adhering to the Constitution, asks Congress for a declaration of war against Germany. Within 4 days approval is granted with minimal dissent from either house of Congress.
April 14	The Committee on Public Information is created with the purpose of influencing the public's opinion towards the war.
June 15	Congress passes the *Espionage Act*, making it illegal to interfere with the draft or overall war effort, encourage others to do the same, or assist the nation's enemies.
June 26	U.S. troops land in France.
July 5	The Postmaster of New York City bans the radical magazine *The Masses* from the mails, but refuses to state the exact reasons. After an injunction was filed was the offending material identified, which eventually led to their indictment under the Acts.
November 2	A second revolution occurs in Russia whereby the Bolsheviks seize control. This sends shock waves around the world, especially as the Bolsheviks would then pull Russia out of the war.

1918

January 18	Wilson presents his *Fourteen Points* plan for the post-war world.
April 15	*The Masses* trial begins resulting in a hung jury.
May 16	Congress strengthens the *Espionage Act* with the *Sedition Act*. In this Act it was illegal to speak out against, or even criticize, the government, whether in word or speech, the

	Constitution, or the armed forces. It was further made illegal to obstruct armed forces recruitment and/or curtail wartime production.
June 30	Socialist leader and oft-presidential candidate Eugene V. Debs is arrested for a speech in Canton, Ohio, whereby he criticized Wilson and the war. While he was sentenced to ten years in prison, President Warren G. Harding commuted the sentence in 1921.
August 1	Scott Nearing is acquitted of violating the Acts.
September	The second trial of *The Masses* begins, resulting in another hung jury and the dropping of charges.
November 11	An armistice is signed, officially ending the war. Germany would later have to sign the "war guilt" clause, taking blame for the war, and begin paying reparations.

1919

January 25	Peace delegates approve the creation of a League of Nations, an organization the U.S. would never join.
March 3	The Supreme Court validates the *Espionage Act* in *Schenck v. United States*, using the doctrine of "clear and present danger." The case is also famous for claiming free speech does not give one the right to falsely yell "fire!" in a crowded theatre to cause a panic.
March 10	Eugene V. Debs' conviction under the Acts for an anti-war speech is upheld in *Debs v. United States*.
June 28	The Treaty of Versailles is signed.
November 10	The *Espionage and Sedition Acts* are again upheld in the Supreme Court in *Abrams v. United States*.
November 19	The U.S. Senate refuses to approve the Treaty of Versailles.
December 22	Carrying 249 deportees, the *USS Buford*, also known as the "Soviet Ark," sets sail from the United States.
	Kate Richards O'Hare is convicted for an anti-war speech.
	After a split from the Socialist Party, both the Communist Labor Party and the Communist Party of the United States are formed in Chicago.

1920

November 2	In a repudiation of Wilsonian Democratic policies, the nation elects Republican Warren G. Harding, ushering a period of isolationism from world affairs. However, the fight against radicalism and those who criticize the American way of life was just beginning.

1921

May 19	The *Emergency Quota Act* is passed placing severe restrictions on immigrations, especially those from Eastern Europe.

1923

June 4	In *Meyer v. Nebraska*, laws banning the teaching of languages other than English is ruled unconstitutional.

1924

May 26   The *National Origins Act* is passed, further strengthening the *Emergency Quota Act*.

1925

June 1   *Pierce v. Society of Sisters* held that the banning of parochial schools is prohibited.

June 8   New York's "criminal anarchy statutes" suppressing radical publications is found valid in *Gitlow v. New York*.

1938

May 26   The House Un-American Activities Committee (HUAC) is created by Congress to investigate, as the name implies, un-American actions taken by those within the country.

1940

June 29   The *Alien Registration Act* (also known as the *Smith Act*) is passed. Besides establishing more requirements on immigrants, it was also made illegal to advocate or teach the overthrow or destruction of any U.S. government by force.

1951

June 4   The *Smith Act* is upheld in the case *Dennis v. United States*.

1956

April 2   In *Pennsylvania v. Nelson*, the Supreme Court overturned Mike Nelson's conviction under a Pennsylvania law banning Communists from employment. This was a technical and not purely legal decision as while the state had a right to protect its sovereignty, federal laws were already in place.

1957

June 17   In *Yates v. United States*, convictions under the *Smith Act* were overturned since those arrested were not actually planning violent acts against any government.

1995

April 19   One of the worst acts committed by domestic terrorists was with the Oklahoma City Bombing, whereby a courthouse building was destroyed due to explosives placed in a van outside. A total of 168 people were killed. One of the conspirators, Timothy McVeigh, was executed for the tragedy.

2001

September 11   The worst terrorist attack on the United States began with the hijacking of four commercial airliners. Two crashed into the World Trade Center Towers, causing their collapse. One flew into the Pentagon. The fourth crashed in a Pennsylvania field when passengers, learning of the other attacks, overpowered the hijackers.

October 26   In the wake of 9/11, the *USA Patriot Act* is passed, providing sweeping powers to agencies to investigate potential terrorist activities.

2016

June 12   The worst mass shooting by a domestic terrorist took place at the Pulse dance club in
                       Orlando, Florida. At the time of writing, Omar Mateen took the lives of 49 and wounded 53
                       more. He was killed in a gun battle with law enforcement.

CHAPTER 1

Introduction

The ability to command the loyalty of citizens is one of the most perplexing problems facing the modern state. Throughout its history, the United States faced a variety of groups and individuals whose ideas were considered anathema to society. Yet, it must be remembered that the nation was built upon political dissent. Whether one believes the original colonies were founded for profits and/or religious freedom, the notion of questioning, or challenging, the philosophical status quo is a recurring theme. During World War I (WWI), this very notion of questioning/challenging what it means to be a loyal and faithful citizen was considered by many to be dangerous to the nation's well-being.

There was never a single unified stream of thought in America, be it political, cultural, religious, or any other treasured idea. After all, what did it mean to be an "American?" "Un-American?" What was, and is, considered to be "traditional American values?" These concepts have, of course, greatly changed over the course of U.S. history. Even the ideas of democracy and republicanism, so deeply entrenched in American culture, are not completely agreed upon. But when the country is in a state of crisis, as with wartime, commanding loyalty in order to achieve the goal of victory takes on many forms. During WWI, the government sought to suppress any perceived dissent, whether in word or deed.

The suspicion of traitorous activities is a preoccupation shared by governments around the world and throughout history. Dealing with such perpetrators arouses passions from all corners of society. On March 25, 1918, California Congressman Julius Kahn exclaimed "When a seditious or traitorous voice is raised here, I hope the law will reach out and grasp the speaker. I hope that we shall have a few prompt hangings."[1] Kahn's statement reflects its period; WWI naturally preoccupied the country, and the Espionage and Seditions Acts[2] prosecuted and persecuted those suspected of subversive activities. For so many across the country, losing their civil liberties became very real. As part of the U.S. government's war effort, the suppression of these liberties—done in the name of national security—was embodied in the Acts where it became illegal to speak out against the war, as well as the war effort. One was expected to act in a manner appropriate to a true patriotic American citizen.

However, what did it mean to be a true American? What were, and are, the criteria? In 1893, Frederick Jackson Turner delivered his infamous paper *The Significance of the Frontier in American History*. In this paper, Turner examined what made Americans so unique. After all, almost all of the nation's original ideas and culture came from abroad. Whether it was the political system, Christianity, English language, or capitalist system, these practices were brought over from Europe. Yet Americans were so different from others, which Turner attributed to the frontier and the constant movement westward. It was out on the frontier, away from the Old World, that settlers and their descendants began to mold these institutions to create a unique society.

But during the 1890s, and well into the twentieth century, the presence of new groups of foreigners was seen as a threat to American institutions. More importantly, these foreigners brought ideas counter to those believed by Americans.

When WWI broke out, even prior to the actual American involvement, many Americans wondered where their loyalty should be: With the country, right or wrong, or, could it be proper to critique the international strife, much less the U.S. involvement? To many, those of foreign birth were suspect enough as they may side with their land of birth. What about those who are natural citizens? If they oppose the war, are they siding with the enemy? This question alone goes back for centuries. But for the U.S. during WWI, this was a truly serious question.

This work is an examination of the Acts and their influence on American society, both during its time and in future decades. While the Acts are not as well known in contemporary times, their effects are still felt. The idea of suppressing anti-war sentiment was even bandied about during the two Gulf Wars of the late twentieth and early twenty-first centuries. Regardless, can any government demand absolute loyalty, no matter what the situation may be? How far can a person go when criticizing the government, whether by word or deed? In times of crisis, a middle ground is not easily discerned, if even at all possible. This book will examine both sides of the issue.

The whole issue of dissent circles around the notion of the First Amendment and the right to free speech. When was the first true test of what constitutes "free speech" in American history? To many, it was the trial of John Peter Zenger in 1735. Granted, while this trial was before the establishment of the United States and/or its Constitution, it nonetheless had a lasting impact.

Zenger (1697–1746) was born in Impflingen in modern-day Germany. He immigrated with his family to New York in 1710. As was common for many young people at the time, Zenger was bound as an apprentice. From 1711 to 1719 he served under William Bradford, a printer. A subsequent joint business venture with Bradford in 1725 was brief, and Zenger would venture out with his own printing business.

In 1733 Zenger became the editor and publisher of the *New-York Weekly Journal*. What brought Zenger into conflict with the law were criticisms of the New York colonial governor William Cosby published in the *Journal*. At that time Cosby was still relatively new in his position, but he quickly made enemies.

Cosby first fought with the colony council about his salary. Then, in order to maintain his dominance over the colony's supreme court, Cosby placed the current chief justice Lewis Morris, who had issued a dissenting opinion in a case against the governor, with James DeLancey, the latter of whom was a member of the royal party and more agreeable to his own policies. These actions would also put Cosby out of favor with the general public as they saw such moves as arbitrary and self-serving.

Zenger certainly shared in the public sentiment, and articles in the *Journal* reflected these views. On the other side of the publication coin was the *New York Gazette*, run by none other than Bradford, Zenger's former mentor and brief business partner. Whereas the *Journal* criticized Cosby and the colonial government, the *Gazette* was the mouthpiece of the royal party.

As the *Journal* continued to print criticisms of the colonial government, Cosby had the British barrister Daniel Horsmanden closely investigate the paper for any potential seditious libel. Based on Horsmanden's findings of seditious libel, two separate grand juries were convened in 1734, both of which would not indict Zenger. Not to be deterred, Cosby used a legal loophole that allowed Zenger to be tried in the absence of a grand jury indictment.

Zenger's first attorneys were William Smith and James Alexander, both of whom were removed from the case, and court, for contempt. Unable to make the £400 bail, Zenger would spend a total of 10 months in jail. When the case (*The Crown v. Zenger*) went to trial in 1735, Zenger was represented by Philadelphia attorney Andrew Hamilton.

It is most likely that Zenger did not write these articles himself; rather, it was by associates working for the *Journal*. But, under the current law, the publisher was held responsible for the content of their prospective news-papers. Hamilton presented the now well-known argument of truth as a defense against libel charges. While Judge DeLancey (Cosby's appointee noted above) refused to allow any evidence to support Hamilton's attempts to prove truth, the jury needed a mere 10 minutes to bring back a not guilty verdict. This was certainly a victory for Zenger, but it is widely believed that the verdict was more of an anti-Cosby statement than anything else.[3]

Despite Zenger's acquittal, the case did not set the legal precedent that many believed it did. However, Hamilton's arguments were the inspiration for many battles to come over the issue of freedom of the press.

The notion of how far the federal government can go in suppressing free speech begins early in the nation's years during the Era of the New Republic (the years following the adoption of the U.S. Constitution). During the sole administration of John Adams, the nation's second president, his political battles with Vice-President Thomas Jefferson became famous. Due to the nature of the presidential electoral system at the time, the idea of a presidential candidate selecting his running mate did not guarantee both would gain office. In the election of 1796, Adams and Jefferson were of different political parties, an extremely new concept and one never repeated, remained unique in terms of presidential administrations.

The political animosity between Adams and Jefferson grew. When combined with the current intense international situations in Europe, all this further contributed to their already strained relationship. The "Quasi-War" with France did much to divide both the government and the nation. Adams favored England, Jefferson favored France. In 1798, Congress passed the Alien and Sedition Acts. With the possibility of an actual war with France, Congress not only extended the period of naturalization (the time in which to become a citizen), but granted the president the authority to order out of the country anyone "suspicious" of being a danger to the country.

While many sections addressed violations of federal law, the most notorious provisions were aimed at the use of free speech. With penalties of $2000 and 2 years in prison, the law aimed to prosecute anyone who published "false, scandalous and malicious writing" against the government, Congress, or the President. It must be noted that the vice-president was not protected from such criticisms, making this office fair game. Out of 25 accused political dissenters, 10 were convicted. When Jefferson took over as president in 1801, he subsequently pardoned those convicted, and their financial penalties were repaid with interest. While this legislation was set to expire by 1801, provisions regarding "alien enemies" still remain in place.[4]

Many people believe that the first real drive to protect America from poisonous and disloyal influences from foreign sources reaches back to the first Age of Reform (c.1820–1850). Beginning while the era of the New Republic was giving way to a settled American system, the first Age of Reform was a precursor to the later Progressive Era (c.1890–1920—to be discussed later). As an American identity grew, so did a growing distrust of new immigrants. During the colonial era, the predominant groups settling the new land were English, French, German, and Scandinavian. However, as the nineteenth century began to unfold, new groups were entering the country, especially the Irish.

The Irish already had a bad reputation, especially among the British or those of British descent. But to the Americans, who were overwhelmingly Protestant, the predominantly Catholic Irish were seen as a threat to American institutions. Calls were made to restrict their entry, as well as those who were also seen an unworthy. American nativism was growing strong. The Know Nothing Party, a political party devoted to nativism and anti-Catholicism, strove to keep the nation pure from undesirable foreign influences. As for its name, supposedly when one was asked about the party, the response was "I know nothing" (although in reality the moniker was true). The party was a failure as it ignored the true main issues of the day, especially slavery.

Along with government actions to counter political dissent, wartime protests were also a part of the nation's history, although not as pronounced as in more contemporary times. During wartime in any country there are bound to be opponents, no matter how small the conflict. Not all were in favor of the Mexican–American War (1846–1848) or the later Spanish–American War (1898), but the first notable anti-protest was during the Civil War with the New York Draft Riots in July, 1863. President Abraham Lincoln and Congress instituted the nation's first ever military draft. Using the Constitutional provision that Congress had the authority to raise and maintain an army, it was argued such a move was legal. This action was also taken by the Confederacy.

Others, however, felt different. Besides believing the draft was not constitutional in any way, other arguments felt this was discriminatory against poorer citizens since a monetary payment could exempt one from the draft. In New York City, not only were these objections prevalent, but so were racist ideas. Led by groups of Irish-Americans, many did not wish to fight in a war that was increasingly becoming solely a slavery issue, something many Northerners felt was none of their business. Some free blacks living in the city were lynched, and there was considerable looting. While this was not a protest specifically against the Civil War, the means by which to conduct the conflict were called into question. Such sentiments were also felt in the Confederacy.[5]

In the post-Civil War decades, a different type of political thinking was gaining momentum. In 1848, Karl Marx and Frederick Engels published *The Communist Manifesto*. While its impact in the U.S. was not immediate, the latter half of the nineteenth century saw the increased presence of Marxist-influenced thinking. As this influence grew, so did the notion that such ideas were "un-American" and went contrary to "traditional" American values.[6]

As the perceived threat grew, so did the reaction. Confrontation was only a matter of time, which eventually came in Chicago in 1886 with the infamous Haymarket Riot. In a well-told story, labor relations in Chicago were strained. After a violent confrontation between police and workers, a protest meeting was called for May 4. Despite its peaceful nature, police raided the meeting, although told by Chicago mayor Carter Harrison not to disturb the event. A still-unknown assailant threw a dynamite bomb, immediately killing one officer. In the subsequent rioting, several people were killed. In November of the following year, four men—all radicals—were hanged in connection with the riot, although there was absolutely no evidence to warrant their conviction.[7]

While the impetus for the protest meeting and subsequent riot initially focused on labor relations, the underlying heart of the matter was the fear of radicalism, real or perceived. In Illinois, the General Assembly cracked down swiftly on these fears with two acts—*The Cole Anti-Boycott* law and the *Merritt Conspiracy* law, both in 1887, and both met with fierce debate. *Cole* struck at removing one of labor's most vital weapons, the boycott, as the name implies. *Merritt* went even further when it came to both actions and free speech. According to the law, if the words of one prompted another to (supposed) illegal action, then both parties were guilty. *Merritt* was eventually repealed while *Cole* lasted for decades, although watered down through court decisions.[8]

Granted, the Chicago incidents were local and not national, but yet they demonstrate an important issue in U.S. legal/political history, and that is how to deal with dissent. A group with placards picketing a courthouse is one instance. A potentially national movement against a policy is another. When combined with those who are/were radical, whether real or perceived, any challenges to the system presented a challenge, and that is, once again, what is the line between civil liberties and national objectives?

When examining this topic, we must first examine the numerous ways it was addressed in scholarly works. In *American Political Prisoners*, Stephen Kohn believes this period as "deliberately ignored." Furthermore, "As a result, a developing human rights movement was uprooted and disposed of in an unmarked grave."[9]

Most people, if not all, begin with Zechariah Chafee's *Free Speech in the United States*. Originally published in 1948, then revised and rewritten under separate titles, over the years, this is a look at the free speech issue from the post-WWI years to World War II.[10] It could be argued that Chafee's liberal view was politically emotional at the time of publication, but it nonetheless provides a view of how such actions were perceived during its time. Chaffee's work remains a staple part of WWI bibliography in contemporary times.

Paul L. Murphy takes a look at the development of the free speech and civil rights issues in *World War I and the Origin of Civil Liberties in the United States.*[11] As Murphy states, "Why had the politics of civil liberties not been a factor in the shaping of public policy in the years prior to 1917?" He also reiterates others in that the U.S. Supreme Court neither addressed nor protected civil liberties during its first 150 years.[12] He furthers points out that "What happened during [WWI] in the civil liberties area was a new and disturbingly different development in American history." As many have noted, prior to the twentieth century, the federal government was not deeply involved in the everyday lives of its citizens; the Progressive Movement produced that change.[13]

Two other older works examine the American domestic scene of WWI: Joan M. Jensen's *The Price of Vigilance*, and Robert Justin Goldstein's *Political Repression in Modern America*. In Jensen's work, she examines the numerous organizations across the country to combat the so-called "German Menace," including groups such as the American Protective League (APL).[14] To Goldstein, "Given the tremendous amount of opposition to American participation in the war, the severe governmental repression which developed did not constitute an irrational response."[15]

David Rabban takes up a theme that Murphy explored, and that is where exactly did the modern version of free speech emerge? As mentioned earlier in this Introduction with the Alien and Sedition Acts and the Zenger case, free speech was not even a legal issue, much less political. Mudslinging political campaigns might have riled a few feathers, but no such incidents ever made their way to the Supreme Court. With the advent of the Progressive Era, this would change. Rabban's *Free Speech in Its Forgotten Years* also takes a look at this point of view. As Rabban states, "The free speech controversies did not spring from a void." And, as Murphy mentions, the Progressive Era was the first real "battleground" for the free speech fight.[16] Rabban also correctly accuses Chafee of ignoring free speech challenges prior to 1917.

There are sources that discuss the Acts from a different focus. Donald G. Donalson's *The Espionage and Sedition Acts of World War I: Using Wartime Loyalty for Revenge and Profit* examines the era from local points of view. While many concentrate on the federal persecution and/or prosecution of the Acts, Donalson looks at how others used the wartime hysteria to harass supposed dissenters. Murphy and Jensen do a brief examination of this issue, while Donalson looks at how many used the times to provide "those with a hidden grudge with the means to accomplish their vengeance," meaning it was easy to accuse one of disloyalty as a way to humiliate one's enemies.[17] Most think of war profiteering as an economic one; while Donalson does not deny this, his view of such profiteering is also one of social and political profit.

Frances H. Early's *A World Without War: How U.S. Feminists and Pacifists Resisted World War I* certainly takes a feminist view of women's resistance towards WWI, but the point of view is more of a twenty-first century focus, rather than that of how women at the time felt during the conflict. Indeed, many of the sentiments may remain the same, but Early's view of how women felt at the time reflect more of how those felt during the two Gulf Wars than those of 1917. Women's rights in the early twentieth century were far less in 1917 than 1997.[18]

Christopher Capozzola's *Uncle Sam Wants You: World War I and the Making of the Modern American Citizen* particularly examines the notion of patriotism. Beginning with the now-iconic symbol of the Uncle Sam character saying "I want YOU," Capozzola argues "When Uncle Sam jabbed his finger at the American public, he pointed out their rights, and he also pointed out who was or who wasn't an American."[19] Although this notion was in place well before the Acts, Cappozzola so adequately describes how even popular culture can, and will, determine who might be perceived as an enemy.

As Nancy Gentile Ford points out in *Issues of War and Peace*, the war

> created a tremendous strain on society, as the nation struggled to balance its democratic principles with its need for a united home front. The failure to do so further divided the country and created a postwar atmosphere that made radicalism, ethnic pride, and pacifism difficult and even unacceptable.[20]

Geoffrey Stone takes this a step further in *Perilous Times: Free Speech in Wartime* when he states "The enemy is more likely to fight fiercely if it is confident and believes its adversary divided and uncertain. Public disagreement during a war can strengthen the enemy's resolve."[21]

While, as stated above, Kohn believes this period to be ignored, what is definitely not known (or, ignored), are the long-term effects of the Acts. As of the time of this writing, the Espionage Act is still on the books. For instance, in 2013 Chelsea (formerly Bradley) Manning was convicted under the Espionage Act for leaking classified documents and was sentenced to 35 years in prison. Edward Snowden, formerly with the Central Intelligence Agency (CIA) and a National Security Agency (NSA) contractor, was under surveillance for also providing classified materials to WikiLeaks, an organization built upon the dissemination of such information. Snowden fled the U.S., and ended up in Russia. Some consider both to be heroes for "telling the truth about this country," while others consider them to be traitors.[22] In either case the issue of free speech was a vital part.

But in the immediate post-WWI years, the American victory did not spell the end of hysteria against radicalism. The two revolutions in Russia in

1917, the second of which saw the Bolsheviks victorious, and pulling that country out of the war, many were afraid such an event might be possible elsewhere. Many Americans did not want to see radicalism erase Americanism, and took steps to prevent it.[23] After the creation of the Communist Party and Communist Labor Party in 1919, government crackdowns against supposed un-American individuals increased. In 1920, A. Mitchell Palmer of the Department of Justice staged a series of raids against political and labor agitators, foreign and domestic, and deported many of those arrested. This is remembered as the First Red Scare.

Although the hysteria of the early 1920s died down, suspicions against perceived un-American activities did not. In 1938 Congress created HUAC—the Houses Un-American Activities Committee, a group whose purpose was clearly in its name. Investigations and hearings targeted those who might fall under that banner, culminating with the Second Red Scare of the 1950s where many targeted individuals and groups lost their civil liberties.

In 1940, just prior to the United States' entry into World War II (WWII), the government passed the Alien Registration Act, more commonly known as the Smith Act. This law strengthened the admission and deportation of aliens. The provisions that are more known made it illegal to teach or advocate the overthrow of the U.S. government, or to join a group that preached such doctrines. As for the ongoing fears of loyalty, one group was especially targeted. When the country eventually entered the conflict, the fear that Japanese Americans would conspire with Japan to bring the country to defeat resulted in the internment of thousands into relocation camps. Their loyalty, as those of German Americans during WWI, was called into question.

The two wars with Iraq stirred similar feelings. The First Persian Gulf War of 1991, and later the Second Persian Gulf War of 2003, which essentially ended in 2013, brought many issues of loyalty to the fore. With the second conflict more of a response to the horrific events of 9/11, the presence of foreigners in the country was an easy way to place blame. More importantly, with the refusal of France to support the second conflict gave way to behavior associated with WWI. As is well known, during WWI many German names for items were changed (i.e. sauerkraut became liberty cabbage), and during the second Persian conflict names such as French Fries became freedom fries. Even President George W. Bush hinted at passing legislation to dissuade dissenters.

All of these occurrences will be discussed in greater detail in the concluding chapters called "Aftermath" and "Legacies." While the debate rages over the line between national security and civil liberties, this era helped to establish a precedent for future actions to curb seemingly un-American activities. And, in the wake of 9/11, the attacks upon any "foreign" influences are under the guise of protecting traditional American values.

Again, the question remains: What are "traditional" American values? What is the meaning of "free speech?" Can either one be regulated, controlled, or simply left alone? When examining the era of the Acts, as many of the above authors mentioned, this was the true beginning of the modern idea of civil rights.

Turner's thesis does not ring true in contemporary times. However, many of his points do have relevance. What does it mean to be an American? While Turner did not address the idea of patriotism, his overall idea will never stop being a part of American culture. Who is an American, and can this person challenge his/her country's policies without being perceived as a threat?

The unique characteristics of American culture began when the first permanent colonies were established during the seventeenth century. What was also established was, as noted above, the idea of political dissent. Upon the American involvement in WWI, these ideas became every bit as important to victory as did military conquests. With the passage of the Acts, WWI became not just a battle between armies, but also between minds.

NOTES

1   "Kahn Would Silence Sedition With Rope," *New York Times*, 25 March 1918, George Creel Papers, Container 19, Manuscript Collection, Library of Congress, Washington, DC.

2   Hereinafter referred to as "the Acts," unless specifically noted, since the two were passed at different times. While this may be the case, they are generally referenced together.

3   For further reading, see Paul Finkelman, *A Brief Narrative of the Case and Tryal of John Peter Zenger: With Related Documents* (New York: Bedford/St. Martin's, 2010); www.nycourts.gov/history/legal-history-new-york/legal-history-eras-01/History_Tryal-John-Peter-Zenger.pdf (accessed December 7, 2015); and William Lowell Putnam, *John Peter Zenger and the Fundamental Freedom* (Flagstaff, AZ: Light Technology Publishing, 1997).

4   For further reading, see Terri Diane Halperin, *The Alien and Sedition Acts of 1798: Testing the Constitution* (Baltimore, MD: Johns Hopkins University Press, 2016); Charles Slack, *Liberty's First Crisis: Adams, Jefferson, and the Misfits Who Saved Free Speech* (New York: Atlantic Monthly Press, 2015).

5   For further reading, see Iver Bernstein, *The New York City Draft Riots: The Significance for American Society and Politics in the Age of the Civil War* (New York: Oxford University Press, 1990); Adrian Cook, *The Armies of the Streets: The New York City Draft Riots of 1863* (Lexington, KY: University Press of Kentucky).

6   These concepts will be further discussed in Chapter 2.

7   See Mitchell Newton-Matza, *Intelligent and Honest Radicals: The Chicago Federation of Labor and the Politics of Progression* (Lanham, MD: Lexington Books, 2013), 22–24.
8   Ibid.
9   Stephen M. Kohn, *American Political Prisoners* (Westport, CT: Praeger, 1994), 1.
10 Zechariah Chafee, *Free Speech in the United States* (Cambridge, MA: Harvard University Press, 1948).
11 Paul L. Murphy, *World War I and the Origin of Civil Liberties in the United States* (New York: W.W. Norton, 1979).
12 Ibid., 9–10.
13 Ibid., 25. The influence of the Progressive Movement will be discussed in Chapter 2.
14 Joan M. Jensen, *The Price of Vigilance* (Chicago, IL: Rand McNally, 1968).
15 Robert Justin Goldstein, *Political Repression in Modern America: 1870s to the Present* (Cambridge: Schenkman Publishing, 1978), 107.
16 David M. Rabban, *Free Speech in Its Forgotten Years* (Cambridge: Cambridge University Press, 1997), 2.
17 Daniel G. Donalson, *The Espionage and Sedition Acts of World War I: Using Wartime Loyalty Law for Revenge and Profit* (El Paso, TX: LFB Scholarly, 2012), 1.
18 Frances H. Early, *A World Without War: How U.S. Feminists and Pacifists Resisted World War I* (Syracuse, NY: Syracuse University Press, 1997).
19 Christopher Capozzola, *Uncle Sam Wants You: World War I and the Making of the Modern American Citizen* (Oxford: Oxford University Press, 2008), 7.
20 Nancy Gentile Ford, *Issues of War and Peace* (Westport, CT: Greenwood Press, 2002), 11.
21 Geoffrey R. Stone, *Perilous Times: Free Speech in Wartime* (New York: W.W. Norton, 2004), 4.
22 As of the time of this writing Snowden was still in Russia.
23 See the chapter "Reformers, Radicals and Socialists" in Mitchell Newton-Matza, Ed., *Jazz Age: People and Perspectives* (Santa Barbara, CA: ABC-CLIO, 2009).

BIBLIOGRAPHY

Bernstein, Iver. *The New York City Draft Riots: The Significance for American Society and Politics in the Age of the Civil War.* New York, NY: Oxford University Press, 1990.
Capozzola, Christopher. *Uncle Sam Wants You: World War I and the Making of Modern American Citizens.* Oxford, UK: Oxford University Press, 2008.
Chafee, Zechariah. *Free Speech in the United States.* Cambridge, MA: Harvard University Press, 1948.
Cook, Adrian. *The Armies of the Streets: The New York City Draft Riots of 1863.* Lexington, KY: University Press of Kentucky, 2014.
Donalson, Daniel G. *The Espionage and Sedition Acts of World War I: Using Wartime Loyalty Laws for Revenge and Profit.* El Paso, TX: LFB Scholarly Publishers, 2012.
Early, Frances H. *A World Without War: How U.S. Feminists and Pacifists Resisted World War I.* Syracuse, NY: Syracuse University Press, 1997.
Finkelman, Paul. *A Brief Narrative of the Case and Tryal of John Peter Zenger: With Related Documents.* New York, NY: Bedford/St. Martin's, 2010.
Ford, Nancy Gentile. *Issues of War and Peace.* Westport, CT: Greenwood Press, 2002.

Goldstein, Robert Justin. *Political Repression in Modern America: 1870 to the Present.* Cambridge, MA: Schenkman, 1978.

Halperin, Terri Diane. *The Alien and Sedition Acts of 1798: Testing the Constitution.* Baltimore, MD: Johns Hopkins University Press, 2016.

Jensen, Joan M. *The Price of Vigilance.* Chicago, IL: Rand McNally, 1968.

Kohn, Stephen M. *American Political Prisoners.* Westport, CT: Praeger, 1994.

Murphy, Paul L. *World War I: The Origin of Civil Liberties in the United States.* New York, NY: W.W. Norton, 1979.

Newton-Matza, Mitchell. *Intelligent and Honest Radicals: The Chicago Federation of Labor and the Politics of Progression.* Lanham, MD: Lexington Books, 2013.

——, Ed. *Jazz Age: People and Perspectives.* Santa Barbara, CA: ABC-CLIO, 2009.

www.nycourts.gov/history/legal-history-new-york/legal-history-eras-01/History_Tryal-John-Peter-Zenger.pdf (accessed December 7, 2015).

Putnam, William Lowell. *John Peter Zenger and the Fundamental Freedom.* Flagstaff, AZ: Light Technology Publishing, 2014.

Rabban, David M. *Free Speech in its Forgotten Years.* Cambridge, UK: Cambridge University Press, 1997.

Slack, Charles. *Liberty's First Crisis: Adams, Jefferson, and the Misfits Who Saved Free Speech.* New York, NY: Atlantic Monthly Press, 2015.

Stone, Geoffrey R. *Perilous Times: Free Speech in Wartime.* New York, NY: W.W. Norton, 2004.

Washington, DC Library of Congress. Manuscript Collections. George Creel Papers.

CHAPTER 2

Origins

The involvement of the United States in WWI was definitely one of the most vital moments in the nation's history that helped solidify its importance in world affairs, especially those dominated by Western powers. This status was a long time in coming. Ever after the 1783 Treaty of Paris officially ended the War of Independence and established the U.S. as an independent country, most, if not all, European nations had two main views of this new entity. First, the U.S. was considered to be a joke, that this new "great experiment" in republicanism would easily self-destruct. Second, there was fear of this very notion of republicanism, that the people could rule themselves might spread. In a continent whose traditions were steeped in monarchies and aristocratic rule, the theory that governments obtained authority from the people (ignoring that such theories had been in existence for centuries) being put into practice might entice their own populations to actively demand the same privileges.

European attitudes towards the U.S. took an interesting turn with the start of the Civil War. Some nations, like Great Britain, France, and many of the Germanic city-states, were amused by the war. How could a nation "conceived in liberty" be fighting among themselves in such a manner? Great Britain and France favored the Southern rebellious states. They not only felt a kinship with the American southern aristocracy, but also wanted to maintain an active trade partnership, especially for the cotton crops. While one could argue the great upheavals of the early nineteenth century throughout Europe, especially the numerous failed revolutions of 1848, might have brought a smile to the faces of Americans who knew these nations looked down upon the U.S., the main European powers stopped just shy of recognizing the Confederacy.[1]

The United States did not become a world power until the Spanish–American War of 1898. When the U.S. defeated Spain it acquired foreign territory, placing them among the Western powers to expand its influence beyond its own borders. This power would continue to grow, and with the start of WWI, courting or discouraging American involvement became a major concern among the warring European powers.

But more was changing among the Western nations than just the United States becoming a world power. In terms of acknowledged mainstream culture, the Victorian Era was coming to an end. Although generally regarded as a specific period in British history, the influences of the Victorian Era could also been seen throughout the Western world. Named after the long reign of Queen Victoria (1837–1901), cultural norms were expected to be followed: proper courtship between men and women (with premarital sexual relations gravely frowned upon), proper use of language, modest wardrobe, and knowing one's place within society. Topics such as sex, birth control, and radical politics were not what would make a decent society.

Of course, these are sweeping generalizations. With the turn of the twentieth century, and Victoria's passing, society was still expected to conform to a moral code, mostly determined by those who considered themselves to be of a higher caliber than ordinary society (even if this "higher caliber" was just as guilty of violating these norms as others). With the growing spread of radical ideologies, so did segments of society normally shut out of the mainstream start to demand equal status. In the U.S., this meant the growing demand for women's rights, and those of African Americans (although that was not the term used to describe the black population at this time). These were seen as a threat to what decent mainstream society held. When WWI broke out, and the eventual entry of the U.S. into the conflict, the need to preserve what was seen as decent and patriotic became a major issue.

What coincides with the end of the Victorian Era is the rise of the Progressive movement. Whereas the former challenged the existing moral code, the latter only accentuated the sweeping changes in American society. Granted, labeling any period is very much subjective. Identifying any changes in any society is precarious at best, much less labeling them, but it can be discerned how the end of the Victorian Era with that of the Progressive very much coincide, and how these contributed to the mindset of the Americans during WWI.

The Progressive Era is usually defined as existing from 1890 through 1920. The year 1920 is, coincidentally, when the election of Warren G. Harding to the presidency marked the end of the WWI Era, and, thus Wilsonian policies that marked that era. However, while the end of the Victorian Era is more equated with sweeping changes taking place in "decent" society, the Progressive Era was far more complex.[2]

The question remains as to how all this ties in WWI and the Acts. Since the end of the American Civil War in 1865, the U.S. industrialized so rapidly the country would not only catch up with other industrialized nations such as England, but surpass them as well. This meant changes in the labor force, as more women, children, and recent immigrants were entering the workforce at wages far below those paid to men. Politics became more complex as big city bosses made a living running the government in ways at times past thought unthinkable. Freed slaves and their descendants fought for their civil rights. Although women were making strides in having a greater participation in society, they were still shut out of meaningful participation, especially the elective franchise. As Steven J. Diner points out, "Many middle class Americans concluded, therefore, that they had lost control of not only their society but of their own lives."[3]

The amount of literature on the Progressive Era is truly voluminous, as are the debates as to such an era even existed, and who even classified as a progressive. Yet such a period can be discerned. Among the topics mentioned above, there were calls for political reform through a civil service exam system, compulsory education, immigration reform, industrial safety inspections, the right to unionize, and checks on how corporations manipulate laws and government officials for their own profit.[4]

When WWI became a reality in 1914, so did the need to realize how much Western society had changed, and was continuing to change. With these changes came challenges to long-standing norms. As mentioned, this meant conducting the war would take more than just a military victory. So came the need to preserve long-standing norms. The Acts would be just one way to do so.

What was not understood by many in the U.S. was how the war itself came to be, and why their involvement needed such stringent measures to keep the population in line. Many still believe it was the assassination of Austrian Archduke Franz Ferdinand to be the cause (this event will be discussed below). It was the catalyst, not the cause. In order to understand the U.S. involvement in WWI, and all its implications, we must also examine what truly led to the conflict. In each one of these cases, there was a basis behind the Acts.[5] For the sake of this work, what follows are the major reasons, starting with the most influential.[6]

NATIONALISM

The idea of nationalism is relatively new in terms of human history. Perhaps it can be argued that with the final years of the Napoleonic Wars, the nature of the Western world changed. Whereas in their current times, people identified themselves by their particular region; i.e. one might not say "I am Italian" but rather, "I am Roman." The same comes from Germany. "I am Bavarian," or "I am Prussian."

As the nineteenth century wore on, and borders were more fixed, so did the idea of one belonging to not only a specific group, but a nation. Yet, nationalism takes three forms, as has been pointed out before: Geographical, political, and cultural. *Geographical* is obvious, for a group of people live within a designated area. *Political* refers to the system of government within which one lives, with *cultural* as the most obvious of all, being shared personal institutions.

Nationalism can encompass any combination of the three terms. But for WWI, these ideals all came together as to promote the idea of one nation being above another. In terms of this war, this meant not only militarily but also ethnically/racially. With Germany being seen as the cause of the war, the notion of defeating the "evil Huns" took on a deeper meaning, especially among the British, who felt their own culture superior in every way (ignoring the fact that several of their monarchs were of German origin). For the U.S., who shared a kinship with England, this would culminate in the Acts in order to preserve national pride.

IMPERIALISM

The nineteenth century is well noted as the Western powers—namely England, France, Germany, and Holland—carved up Africa and Asia for their own benefits. With the Industrial Revolution in full swing, so did the thirst of empire, raw materials, and new markets. With the race for empire came even further competition between these nations. When the U.S. acquired the Philippines, as well as areas in the Caribbean, she entered the fray. This was not just limited to Africa and Asia, for Austria's annexation of Balkan territory angered many. The need to protect the acquired (stolen?) territories, while attempting to add more area, would increase tensions. What this would lead to is detailed below.

ARMS RACE

Many do not realize that the nuclear arms race of the twentieth century was not the first time an arms race occurred. With all the advances and marvels of the newly industrialized world, and any of its drawbacks, came the ability to create even stronger military capabilities. This was not just in the form of improved firearms and other weaponry, but also in terms of transportation as iron ships replaced wooden military vessels. The need to defend colonies sparked the need to stockpile as much materiel as possible, and be prepared to fight at a moment's notice.

ALLIANCE SYSTEM

While this is probably the most well known of all the causes, it is placed fourth because of the influence the first three would have on this reason. While France and England have a history of fighting each other, they nevertheless had a defense agreement. Germany and Austria share a long, shared bond (and not just ethnically), and Russia felt itself the defender of the Slavic race. When the wheels of war were put into motion, so were the expectations that one nation would have from another.

RACIAL/ETHNIC TENSIONS

It could be argued this would fall under *Nationalism*, but the racial and ethnic tensions existing in Europe at the time, especially within the Austria-Hungary empire, was an important reason. When the Ausgleich of 1867 formally created Austria-Hungary, many of the minority groups within the empire wished for the types of concessions and privileges won by the Hungarians (also known as Magyars). Many groups were happy to remain within the empire, just desiring autonomy. In the case of the Serbs within the empire, their desire to create a yugo-slav, or south Slavic state, along with the territory of Serbia was enough to commit murder. And, in playing along with nationalism, Eastern Europeans in general were looked down upon by other Western nations, believing these people to be inferior.

As it is believed that Franz Ferdinand's murder was the cause of WWI, many also believe that it was the sinking of the Lusitania in 1915 that brought the U.S. into the war (to be discussed below). Although these tragic events were indeed true, they have also taken on a mythical status. Keeping the myths in mind, it is important now to trace what exactly led to what would be dubbed "The Great War."

On June 28, 1914, Serbian nationalists in Bosnia celebrated Vidovdan, or, St. Vitus' Day, commemorating the event in which the medieval Serbian empire was destroyed by the Turks. On this same day, Archduke Franz Ferdinand, heir to the Habsburg throne, visited Sarajevo, the capital of Bosnia. By the end of the day Franz Ferdinand was dead, slain by a Serbian-sponsored terrorist. The assassin never dreamed his action would lead to a world war.

The notion to assassinate Franz Ferdinand was a curious one. He actually supported a third wing to the empire of the Slavic groups. This was not out of love of the Slavs but rather to counter the Magyar portion of the empire. The current emperor, Franz Josef, was slow to appoint Franz Ferdinand as heir. First, the emperor was not receptive to the progressive ideals of his nephew. Second, Franz Ferdinand had a morganatic marriage to Sophie Chotek, which would disrupt the royal bloodline; and third, Franz Ferdinand had tuberculosis, which the emperor also used as an excuse.

When Franz Ferdinand announced his visit to observe military maneuvers, many members of the Habsburg court expressed disagreement. They felt he was exposing himself and his wife (with whom he was traveling) to danger, citing the high tensions in the area. General Oskar Potiorek, the Habsburg-appointed governor of Bosnia, welcomed him eagerly. At first the trip went well. The welcome in Sarajevo was warm all around. Sophie remarked that all of the fears were groundless; she thought her husband was loved.

Several events were scheduled for June 28. First, Franz Ferdinand was to give a speech at the city hall. Along the way he was in a parade, riding in an open car alongside his wife. While the procession moved along, a young man named Vaso Cubrilovic stepped out of the crowd and threw a grenade, which bounced off the Archduke's car and rolled under the next, where it blew up. Though Franz Ferdinand and Sophie were not hurt, they were blood stained and quite shaken. Cubrilovic swallowed an inffective cyanide capsule, then jumped into the Miljacka river. Despite his efforts, he was captured.

Franz Ferdinand insisted on proceeding, and, to be expected, in a bad mood. In front of the crowd at his city hall address, he turned to Sarajevo mayor Fehim Effendi Curcic and said "Mr. Mayor, one comes here for a visit and is received with bombs! It is outrageous!"[7] After the speech, the parade drove back in the same direction from whence it came, a move many felt was suicidal. Some, like Potiorek, felt a second attack was unlikely.

At one point in the second parade there was apparently some confusion, and the parade turned the wrong direction. The procession was stopped and began to back up. As this occurred, a young Bosnian named Gavrilo Princip stepped forward, and "at a distance of not more than five feet, fired twice. One bullet pierced Franz Ferdinand's neck, while the other entered Sophie's abdomen."[8] Before the staff could transport the royal couple to the governor's house for medical treatment, Franz Ferdinand and Sophie were dead.[9]

After the assassination, seven people involved were arrested, one of which was Princip. All were inhabitants of Bosnia; six were Serbs, one was Muslim. All were young men, either in their teens or early twenties (Princip was 19). All were students belonging to a group called "Young Bosnia." All were pro-Serbian Jugo-Slavs.

Investigations showed that the weapons provided for the murder were supplied by Serbia. The conspirators were shown to be in contact with Serbian Colonel Dragutin Dimitrijevic, more commonly known as Apis. Apis was the head of a secret group whose official name was "Union or Death," but more popularly called the "Black Hand." Austria knew the assassination was connected with the Serbian government, but how deeply was obscure.

What is usually not known is that Franz Josef did not care much that the heir was assassinated. When a member of the royal family dies, there are different periods of mourning. The emperor proclaimed a mere one month of mourning. Yet how did this murder escalate to the point of worldwide catastrophe?

While Serbian officials were willing to allow Austria part of the assassination investigation, they still demanded their sovereignty. Austria turned to Germany, who issued the infamous blank *cheque*, stating they would support Austria. After Serbia's rejection of Austria's ultimatum, troops from both Austria and Russia began to mobilize. Austria would declare war on Serbia, with then German and French forces mobilizing. After numerous rejected ultimatums and failed diplomacy, Austria and Germany became embroiled with Russia, England and France, with many declarations of war thrown about.

How would this influence the U.S.? When the war broke out, President Woodrow Wilson took a neutral stance. However, there was no denying the long, deep ties that the U.S. has with England, American Revolution or not.

[Thomas] Woodrow Wilson (1856–1924)

His 1916 re-election slogan "He Kept Us Out of War" was soon viewed as one of the greatest lies in a president campaign. The twenty-eighth president of the United States, his two terms in office are marked by raging contradictions. He wanted to make the world safe for democracy, yet imposed not just racial discrimination in the armed forces and government, but led a charge to suppress free speech as never before. A well-educated man, he wrote numerous pieces, served as governor of New Jersey, and would eventually become president of Princeton University. Elected president on the Democratic ticket in 1912, he appeared as a reformer fitting in well with the Progressive Movement. When WWI broke out, he claimed to maintain neutrality, although the nation's heart was with Great Britain and France (the feelings towards Russia were still uncertain). His actions towards political dissent once the nation entered the conflict were swift. One of the issues that concerned Wilson was the post-war world, with his proposed *Fourteen Points* as the blueprint for such a world, including the formation of a League of Nations. Upon the war's conclusion came the Paris Peace Conference of 1919. Although declining in health, he still traveled to France. At home, he did believe in women's suffrage, but acceded to members of his party who were opposed. He would eventually succumb to his ill health and died in Washington, DC.

The Germans were seen as the villains, desperate to take over the world (although Germany had nothing to do with the start of the war). The "evil Huns" were set on death and destruction, while decent societies such as England, from whom this country borrowed so much, were cultured, civilized people.

Despite the ties with England, American neutrality was violated by both sides of the European conflict. It can easily be argued that if one is trading with my enemy, I have the right to step in and stop it. Many also believe it was Germany's sinking of the *Lusitania* in 1915 to be the reason behind the U.S. entry into the war. In reality, Germany warned Americans not to board the vessel as it was carrying war munitions (it was). Some 124 Americans died in the sinking, and Germany issued an apology for this fact. It was two events that especially prompted the U.S. involvement: The infamous Zimmerman Telegrams, and the renewed use of unrestricted submarine warfare.

An intercepted telegram from Germany to Mexico agreed that should the latter enter the war, there was a promise to restore territory taken from the Mexican–American War of the 1840s. The other was Germany's continued use of unrestricted submarine warfare. The U.S. severed diplomatic ties with Germany. After Wilson ran on a re-election program in 1916 of "He Kept Us Out of War," in April of 1917, Congress approved his war message, with the official declaration on April 6.

Now the Americans were fighting the "evil Huns." There was much to consider in how to proceed. The military, obviously, needed to mobilize as soon as possible. At the time of the war declaration, approximately 200,000 men were in the army, a number that would expand to over four million, over half of whom were drafted.[10]

With the military deployment came the age-old realization that the home front must be maintained as well. This meant hearts and minds. There were three specific groups immediately thought to be suspect: Immigrants, radicals, and overall war dissenters, especially pacifists. These are not mutually exclusive groups; one could belong to a single label, or identify with any combination of the three. True Americans must be on the lookout for such deviants. As Joan M. Jensen points out, when Wilson signed the war declaration, "the volunteer home front army was already in arms."[11] But, as Steven J. Diner points out,

> Yet despite outward displays of patriotism and commitment to the mobilization effort, American entrance into the European war escalated long-standing conflicts and social strains . . . Against this backdrop, reformers and intellectuals fought to expand the role of government and argued over the ways in which it could restore individual autonomy and empower citizens to direct the nation's future.[12]

Immigrants were the easiest of targets, especially those who most recently arrived in the country. How much loyalty did they still have to their homeland? Could they be trusted to support their new country? It is well noted that German agents approached those from countries such as Ireland and India (if not directly in those lands), both of whom were under British dominations. Support for the Axis cause would not only weaken England's resolve, but the idea of possible immediate independence was a strong incentive. More importantly, those of German decent, whether recent immigrants or even third-generation U.S. born, were under suspicion of wanting to undermine the American war effort. This could go anywhere from refusing to fight to sabotaging the industrial aspect. As Wilson said, "For us there is but one choice. We have made it. Woe be to the man or group of men that seeks to stand in our way in this day of high resolution."[13]

The radical segment was a bit more difficult to identify. After all, what does a radical look like? Well-known radicals such as the Russian immigrant Emma Goldberg, or the American born John Reed could easily by spotted, but what of the others? As with recent immigrants, the easiest people to identify are obviously those who are members of a radical group, such as the Industrial Workers of the World (IWW) and the Socialist Party (SP). When the war initially broke out, Marxist-based groups believed it was the vindication of Marxist theory, that the working classes would refuse to fight for the rich, and that the proletariat would rise up in revolt of a capitalist war. However, it would not be as easy as that. Radicals were faced with a difficult choice: Support the U.S. war effort and be accused of not adhering to their own philosophy, or refuse to support the war, and face persecution.

War dissenters were also seen as a threat to the involvement, especially pacifists. Many pacifists used the image of Jesus Christ as a model, and that is to harm no one, and love everybody. Even for the non-religious (of whatever faith they might be), the idea of senseless slaughter would produce no results other than worldwide misery. If war dissent was too widespread, it was feared by some that those who would refuse to register for the draft would result in smaller armed forces, thus leaving the nation open to potential defeat.

But there was valid reason to be concerned about dissent, especially as the first years of the war—before the U.S. entry—were devastating. As Geoffrey R. Stone relates, "The carnage was horrifying," with hundreds of thousands of European troops already dead within 2 years, and without gaining any ground. Furthermore,

Between the outbreak of war in Europe and the decision of the United States to enter the conflict in the spring of 1917, there was continuing debate about the nation's best course of action. Most Americans

> believed that the war in Europe did not implicate vital interests of the
> United States . . . A key question in World War I was whether the United
> States could punish public opposition to the war because it might sap
> the nation's resolve and thus the war effort.[14]

Nancy Gentile Ford takes this a step further by stating "The pervasive class, ethnic, and ideological diversity of American Society, along with the unpopular nature of World War I, brought a new crisis to the United States."[15]

As with the Progressive Era in the country, there are also innumerable works dealing with the military portion of America's involvement in WWI.[16] There is no need to recount that aspect of the war years here. Wilson was not going to tolerate dissent, stating "it will be dealt with a firm hand of stern repression."[17] He also felt that the strong presence of the foreign born population, whether citizens or not, would support their former countries against the United States. Such actions would begin very quickly to try and curb potentially harmful activities.[18]

Prior to the passage of the Acts, Wilson used his executive authority in other ways. First, a February, 1917 law made issuing any threats against the president illegal. Second, using the Alien Enemies Act of 1798 (see Chapter 1), all alien enemies would be arrested. Wilson would strengthen this later by requiring any Germans the age of 14 and older to register, restricted their freedom of mobility, and prohibited them from being near military posts and Washington, DC. The fear of anyone of German descent was escalating very quickly.[19]

Congress began considering legislation concerning dissent in just a little over two weeks after war was declared. It must be noted that such debates were not one-sided against dissent. "In fact, Congress took its constitutional responsibilities quite seriously and expressly rejected several key provisions proposed by the Wilson administration."[20] One such provision especially concerned press censorship. Many felt this was too strong and provided the president with far too much power. The media especially protested this provision. Besides using free speech arguments, to censor the press would limit the right of people to know what was going on, and, thus "seeking to deprive them of the means of forming intelligent opinion."[21] By a vote of 39 to 38, the Senate removed that portion of the bill. Wilson still insisted it was necessary to have such authority, but his pleas would not persuade Congress to reinsert it.

Despite being defeated with the rejection of the press censorship, on June 15, 1917, Wilson signed the Espionage Act.[22] This Act itself was not one solid bill when introduced. Rather, it was more of a conglomeration of several bills. Again, its promoters within Congress argued that any decent, patriotic, law-abiding citizen had nothing to fear, that the country was being protected from those who wished to cause harm. Its opponents feared that once such powers were granted, thereby trampling on civil rights, even harsher legislation would follow.

Aimed at treasonous and disloyal activities, the Espionage Act provided two sets of severe penalties. The first imposed a $10,000 fine and 20 years imprisonment for anyone found guilty of aiding the enemy, obstructing recruiting (especially the draft), or causing or promoting insubordination, disloyalty, or refusal of duty within the armed forces. A maximum 30-year sentence or the possibility of the death sentence would be for those who provided information that would interfere with armed forces activities, or encouraged the nation's enemy to succeed. Furthermore, the Postmaster General was given the authority to exclude from the mails any materials believed to treasonous or seditious (See Chapter 3 for examples).

On October 6, 1917, Congress passed the Trading with the Enemy Act.[23] This act prohibited any commerce with enemy nations (which in itself is a reasonable law, especially to curb smuggling), but with their associates as well. The president was also given the right to impose an embargo on any imports, and to censor materials passing between the U.S. and foreign nations. Foreign language newspapers had to receive Post Office approval before using the mails. The Office of Alien Property Custodian could seize property in the U.S. held by those living in enemy countries.

While the Trading with the Enemy Act was not directly related to the Espionage Act, it was in 1918 that Wilson and Congress went even further. In what is generally known as the Sedition Acts, this law was actually a series of amendments to the Espionage Act. Passed on May 16, 1918, this was meant, and used, to strengthen the earlier law.

The Sedition Act[24] also provided severe penalties, as did the Espionage Act. In this case, those convicted would receive prison sentences from 5 to 20 years for making or conveying false statements interfering with the prosecution of the war. It also went after those who willfully employed "disloyal, profane, scurrilous, or abusive language" about the American government, the constitution, the flag, and/or the armed forces. It also prohibited curtailing production of war materials, or to encourage or teach in any manner performing such acts. And, as with the Espionage Age, the Postmaster General could refuse to allow any materials through the mails that met these criteria.

Once again, Congress found itself in fierce debate. While the usual arguments were made, this time the debate was even more acrimonious. The wording of the act was especially volatile, and even more explicit than the first law.

Members of Congress from both major political parties agreed on the dangers of the extreme wording. As to be expected, Wilson backed this latest legislation. While he did not get the press censorship provision he wanted in the first act, this new piece gave those who backed his policies a bit more satisfaction. And a bit more power than was ever imagined.

While it is generally believed that intense Congressional debate often runs along party lines, members of both parties argued vigorously for and against. As to be expected, members of the Wilson administration supported the bill as it would provide extra powers denied in the Espionage Act. However, many Democrats, Wilson's political party, felt the wording of both Acts was true and strong, and some even welcomed outright criticism as a way of fostering healthy debate. Other Democrats feared that prosecuting war dissenters would only hurt the party and administration. In the mid-term elections of 1918, the Democrats lost quite a few seats in both the state and federal government.

While in contemporary times Republicans are thought of as the conservative party, during the WWI era they were still thought by many to be the party of progression. Former Republican president Theodore Roosevelt was opposed to Sedition Act, as were prominent Republicans Hiram Johnson and Henry Cabot Lodge. But as Geoffrey Stones points out, "almost every member of Congress found it necessary to proclaim his loyalty to the nation and his disdain for anyone who might harbor doubts about the American cause." Furthermore, Stone quotes Lodge as saying "I have become a little weary of having Senators get up here and say to those of us who happen to think a word had better be changed," and that they "are trying shelter treason." Stone quotes Johnson as saying "that any person who does 'not subscribe instanter' to every effort to suppress dissent [is] . . . an enemy of the country."[25]

However, despite fierce debate, the Sedition Act passed without a problem. Senator William Borah believed it was a "drastic law" but he wanted to prevent "things far worse."[26] In the House of Representatives, the vote was 293 to 1, with Meyer London of New York casting the only dissenting vote. In the Senate the vote was 48 to 26. Naturally, Wilson signed the Sedition Act into law. What must be noted is that the Sedition Act itself was passed into law when the ending of the war was just only a matter of months away.

Now came the task of enforcing the Acts. One person who especially relished in going after dissenters was Postmaster Albert S. Burleson. The Justice Department, of course, would be involved, although some feared the War Department would gain considerable power in participating with prosecutions. Another prominent individual utilizing the Acts was George Creel, who would be known as leading the Committee on Public Information (all these will be discussed in better detail in Chapter 3).

George Creel (1876–1953)

Creel's participation during the WWI era was heading up the United States Committee on Public Information, created by President Wilson. Described as a propaganda machine, Creel made no bones about not having an open mind. Born in Missouri, he worked as a writer in various capacities, especially in journalism. Working for Wilson's re-election in 1916, he pitched an idea to the President for how to handle the press, resulting in his appointment. This propaganda was not just limited to cartoons and the printed word, but fiery speakers who drummed up support for the war effort. While Creel certainly had strong opinions, he did not support extreme press censorship. After the war Creel continued to write, and even tried to run for California governor against Socialist writer Upton Sinclair as a Democrat, but lost that contest.

As mentioned in Chapter 1, Daniel G. Donalson's examination of the Acts takes on a different viewpoint. As Donalson points out, the Acts served as a platform for people to perform selfish, personal goals.[27] Regardless if there was any overt cooperation between government and private groups, with the Acts in full force, it was a dangerous time to be "different."

The United States was starting to fully exercise its place as a world power by entering WWI. When U.S. troops landed in France, many Americans felt they were repaying a debt to the French from their help during the Revolutionary War. But there was another front to the war, and that was the one at home. Dissenters were not going down easily without a fight. And the fight was just beginning. As John A. Saltmarsh writes, "In New York City, so many dissenters who took to the streets to protest the war were jailed that [the Socialist paper] *The Call* mused whether the prison on Blackwell Island might request a local Socialist party charter."[28]

The entry into the war was just beginning. And so was the actual attack on dissenters, real or perceived. The times were about to get even more dangerous.

NOTES

1   For readings about Europe and the U.S. Civil War, see Don H. Doyle, *The Cause of All Nations: An International History of the American Civil War* (New York: Basic Books, 2015); Amanda Foreman, *A World on Fire: Britain's Crucial Role in the American Civil War* (New York: Random House, 2010); and Phillip E. Myers, *Caution and Cooperation: The American Civil War in British–American Relations* (Kent, OH: Kent State University Press, 2008).

2   In addition to works listed below, also see Michael McGerr, *A Fierce Discontent: The Rise and Fall of the Progressive Movement, 1870–1920* (Oxford, UK: Oxford University Press, 2003); John Whiteclay Chambers II, *The Tyranny of Change:*

America in the Progressive Era, 1890–1920 (New York: St. Martins, 1992); Nell Irwin Painter, *Standing Armageddon: A Grassroots History of the Progressive Era* (New York: W.W. Norton, 2008).

3   Steven J. Diner, *A Very Different Age: Americans in the Progressive Era* (New York: Hill & Wang, 1998), 6.

4   Besides Diner's work, also see Eric Goldman, *Rendezvous with Destiny: A History of Modern American Reform* (Chicago, IL: Ivan R. Dee, 2001); William Loren Katz and Jacqueline Hunt Katz, *Making Our Way: America at the Turn of the Century in the Words of the Poor and Powerless* (New York: Dial Press, 1975); and William L. O'Neil, *The Progressive Years: America Comes of Age* (New York: Dodd, Mead & Company, 1975).

5   This list may not be considered comprehensive by some. Indeed, there might very well be smaller, and lesser influential, reasons for WWI, but these are generally acknowledged to be the major causes.

6   This list is a composite of various theories behind the causes of WWI.

7   Quoted in Joachim Remak, *Sarajevo* (New York: Criterion Books, 1959), 130.

8   Ibid., 137.

9   For further readings on the assassination see Charles River Editors, *The Assassination of Archduke Franz Ferdinand: The History and Legacy of the Event That Triggered World War I* (CreateSpace Independent Publishing Platform, 2014); Paul Ham, *1914: The Assassination of World War I* (RHC eBooks, 2014); Greg King and Sue Woolmans, *The Assassination of the Archduke: Sarajevo 1914 and the Romance that Changed the World* (New York: St. Martins, 2013; and Richard Ned Lebow, *Archduke Franz Ferdinand Lives!: A World Without World War I* (New York: St. Martins, 2014).

10   For some addition information on preparedness, see David M. Kennedy, *Over Here: The First World War and American Society* (Oxford, UK: Oxford University Press, 2004).

11   Joan M. Jensen, *The Price of Vigilance* (Chicago, IL: Rand McNally, 1968), 31.

12   Diner, 233–234.

13   As quoted in Harry N. Scheiber, *The Wilson Administration and Civil Liberties, 1917–1921* (Ithaca, NY: Cornell University Press, 1960), 27.

14   Geoffrey R. Stone, *Perilous Times: Free Speech in Wartime: From the Sedition Acts to the War on Terrorism* (New York: W.W. Norton, 2005), 136–138.

15   Nancy Gentile Ford, *Issues of War and Peace* (Westport, CT: Greenwood Press, 2002), 177.

16   For some good works, see Edwin Howard Simmons and Joseph H. Alexander, *Through the Wheat: The U.S. Marines in World War I* (Annapolis, MD: Naval Institute Press, 2008); Justus D. Doenecke, *Nothing Less than War: A New History of America's Entry into World War I* (Lexington, KY: University of Kentucky Press, 2011); and Edwin M. Coffman, *The War to End All Wars: The American Military Experience in World War I* (Lexington, KY: University of Kentucky Press, 1998).

17   Quoted in Stone, 137.

18   A good source for suppressing dissent is Jesse Walker, *The United States of Paranoia: A Conspiracy Theory* (New York: HarperCollins, 2013).

19   For additional information on how this affected Germans in the U.S. see Robert Justin Goldstein, *Political Repression in Modern America: From 1870 to 1976* (Urbana, IL: University of Illinois Press, 2001).

20   Stone, 146.
21   American Newspaper Publishers' Association, quoted in Stone, 147.
22   *Espionage Act*, Pub. L. 65–24, 40 Stat. 217, 1917.
23   *Trading with the Enemy Act*, 40 Stat. 411, 1917.
24   *Sedition Act*, Pub. L. 65–150, 40 Stat. 553, 1918.
25   As quoted in Stone, 186.
26   Ibid., 187.
27   Daniel G. Donalson, *The Espionage and Sedition Acts of World War I: Using Wartime Loyalty Laws for Revenge and Profit* (El Paso, TX: LFB Scholarly Publishers, 2012), 1.
28   John A. Saltmarsh, *Scott Nearing: The Making of a Homesteader* (White River Junction, VT: Chelsea Green Publishing, 1998), 147.

BIBLIOGRAPHY

Chambers II, John Whiteclay. *The Tyranny of Change: America in the Progressive Era, 1890–1920*. New York: St. Martins, 1992.

Charles River Editors, *The Assassination of Archduke Franz Ferdinand: The History and Legacy of the Event That Triggered World War I*. CreateSpace Independent Publishing Platform, 2014.

Coffman, Edwin M. *The War to End All Wars: The American Military Experience in World War I*. Lexington, KY: University of Kentucky Press, 1998.

Diner, Steven J. *A Very Different Age: Americans in the Progressive Era*. New York, NY: Hill & Wang, 1998.

Doenecke, Justus D. *Nothing Less than War: A New History of America's Entry into World War I*. Lexington, KY: University of Kentucky Press, 2011.

Donalson, Daniel G. *The Espionage and Sedition Acts of World War I: Using Wartime Loyalty Laws for Revenge and Profit*. El Paso, TX: LFB Scholarly Publishers, 2012.

Doyle, Don H. *The Cause of All Nations: An International History of the American Civil War*. New York: Basic Books, 2015.

Espionage Act, Pub. L. 65–24, 40 Stat. 217, 1917.

Foreman, Amanda. *A World on Fire: Britain's Crucial Role in the American Civil War*. New York: Random House, 2010.

Ford, Nancy Gentile. *Issues of War and Peace*. Westport, CT: Greenwood Press, 2002.

Goldman, Eric. *Rendezvous with Destiny: A History of Modern American Reform*. Chicago, IL: Ivan R. Dee, 2001.

Goldstein, Robert Justin. *Political Repression in Modern America: From 1870 to 1976*. Urbana, IL: University of Illinois Press, 2001.

Ham, Paul. *1914: The Assassination of World War I*. RHC eBooks, 2014.

Jenson, Joan M. *The Price of Vigilance*. Chicago, IL: Rand McNally, 1968.

Katz, William Loren and Jacqueline Hunt Katz. *Making Our Way: America at the Turn of the Century in the Words of the Poor and Powerless*. New York: Dial Press, 1975.

Kennedy, David M. *Over Here: The First World War and American Society*. Oxford, UK: Oxford University Press, 2004.

King, Greg and Sue Woolmans, *The Assassination of the Archduke: Sarajevo 1914 and the Romance that Changed the World*. New York: St. Martins, 2013.

Lebow, Richard Ned. *Archduke Franz Ferdinand Lives!: A World Without World War I.* New York: St. Martins, 2014.

McGerr, Michael. *A Fierce Discontent: The Rise and Fall of the Progressive Movement, 1870–1920.* Oxford, UK: Oxford University Press, 2003.

Myers, Phillip E. *Caution and Cooperation: The American Civil War in British–American Relations.* Kent, OH: Kent State University Press, 2008.

O'Neil, William L. *The Progressive Years: America Comes of Age.* New York: Dodd, Mead & Company, 1975.

Painter, Nell Irwin. *Standing Armageddon: A Grassroots History of the Progressive Era.* New York: W.W. Norton, 2008.

Peterson, H.C. and Gilbert C. Fite. *Opponents of War, 1917–1918.* Westport, CT: Greenwood Press, 1957; reprint 1986.

Remak, Joachim. *Sarajevo.* New York: Criterion Books, 1959.

Saltmarsh, John A. *Scott Nearing: The Making of a Homesteader.* White River Junction, VT: Chelsea Green Publishing, 1998.

Scheiber, Harry N. *The Wilson Administration and Civil Liberties, 1917–1921.* Ithaca, NY: Cornell University Press, 1960.

Sedition Act, Pub. L. 65–150, 40 Stat. 553, 1918.

Simmons, Edwin Howard and Joseph H. Alexander. *Through the Wheat: The U.S. Marines in World War I.* Annapolis, MD: Naval Institute Press, 2008.

Stone, Geoffrey R. *Perilous Times: Free Speech in Wartime: From the Sedition Acts of 1798 to the War on Terrorism.* New York: W.W. Norton, 2005.

Trading with the Enemy Act, 40 Stat. 411, 1917.

Walker, Jesse. *The United States of Paranoia: A Conspiracy Theory.* New York: HarperCollins, 2013.

CHAPTER 3

Persecution or Prosecution?

If anything challenges the notion of patriotism, it is wartime. While war protests would become more plentiful, and, to many segments of society, more acceptable, such behavior was not tolerated during WWI. The debate over the Acts raged, so did what labels to assign to those who opposed the moves of the governments, state and federal. Supporters of the Acts considered the opposition to be revolutionary; the opponents would argue they were preserving freedom.

The love for one's country can take many forms. The oft-used phrases "My country, right or wrong," and/or "Love it or leave it" have been used innumerable times through this nation's history. With the prosecution of the Acts came a type of super-patriotism by many segments of society not previously seen. As stated earlier, Daniel Donalson argues how the Acts were used by individuals who "were able to engineer accusations of disloyalty in order to use the overwhelming power of the federal government to complete *highly personal* goals."[1] Christopher Capozzola mentions that

> President Woodrow Wilson dismissed pacifists in a wartime speech before the American Federation of Labor (AFL), noting that "what I am opposed to is not the feeling of the pacifists, but their stupidity. My heart is with them, but my mind has a contempt for them."[2]

But what of the prosecutions within their own context? Elizabeth Stevenson points out that "If the laws had been interpreted narrowly, they might have been argued against as an infringement of freedom." She further goes on to quote Sir Frederick Pollock from a letter he wrote to Oliver Wendell Holmes: "It puzzles me that a special act of Congress should be necessary to make seditious denunciation of the Government and incitements to rebellions in time of war, offenses of the same kind."[3]

Robert Goldstein points out that:

> Altogether, over twenty-one hundred were indicted . . . invariably for statements of opposition to the war rather than for any overt acts, and over one thousand were convicted. Over one hundred were sentenced to jail terms of ten years or more. Not a single person was ever convicted for actual spy activities.[4]

Keeping these ideas in mind, it is now time to examine some of the prosecutions under the Acts.

One of the most famous (infamous?) of all the trials under the Acts was with the prosecution of the radical magazine *The Masses*. As noted in Chapter 1, much scholarship over the past years has focused on the individual experiences. What makes *The Masses* so interesting and so unique? While maybe its experiences under the Acts were not necessarily unique, the trials of *The Masses* certainly provided a type of entertainment, although those up on charges did not feel that way.

Several works examine this case from more basic angles. Leslie Fishbein's *Rebels in Bohemia* holds the affair as something rather unimportant to some of the defendants. While this is true to a point, being on trial was far more complex, and she bases much of her account of the trial on the words of Louis Untermeyer, a *Masses* contributor and witness at the trial.[5] John E. Hart's book *Floyd Dell*, a biography of one of the defendants, the trial appears only as an inconvenience, referring to the ordeal as a "grim joke."[6]

In order to understand fully the problems faced by *The Masses* under the Acts, we need to understand what the magazine itself experienced. *The Masses* was originally founded in 1911 by Piet Vlag, a Dutch restaurant owner. It was not a profit-making magazine, relying on cash donations from rich patrons, as well as donations of time and creativity from its staff. Untermeyer remembers sending Max Eastman a note which read "Dear Eastman: We have just elected

Floyd Dell (1887–1969)

Like Eastman, Dell was a central part of the trial of *The Masses*. Also like Eastman, Dell was a prolific writer, producing works in numerous genres, including the Broadway comedy *Little Accident* in 1928 (and later made into a film). Dell was born in Barry, Illinois, moving to Iowa, eventually falling into a journalist career that found fruit when he moved to Chicago. It was in this city that he started to blossom as a leading thinker in social activism. Moving to New York, he became managing editor of *The Masses*, finding himself on trial for violating the Acts. After both trials resulted in mistrials, Dell would resume his extensive writing career until his death in Bethesda, Maryland.

you editor of *The Masses* at no salary per annum."[7] Eastman himself wrote that "I'm going to find money to pay me the beginnings of a salary on The Masses [sic] or quit it."[8] Dell, however, was more adamant about receiving pay. "I expect to be paid whether there's money there or not. The first week when my cheque doesn't come, I won't say anything. The second week I won't say anything either, but I won't be there."[9]

The Masses was indeed a radical publication. By its own admission it was:

A REVOLUTIONARY AND NOT A REFORM MAGAZINE. A MAGAZINE WITH A SENSE OF HUMOR AND NO RESPECT FOR THE RESPECTABLE. FRANK, ARROGANT, IMPERTINENT, SEARCHING FOR THE TRUE CAUSES: A MAGAZINE DIRECTED AGAINST RIGIDITY AND DOGMA WHEREVER IT IS TO BE FOUND: PRINTING WHAT IS TOO NAKED OR TRUE FOR A MONEY-MAKING PRESS: A MAGAZINE WHOSE FINAL POLICY IS TO DO AS IT PLEASES AND CONCILIATE NOBODY, NOT EVEN ITS READERS.

The Masses was indeed against all types of rigidity. Even within its own circle members of the Left were confused as to what the magazine was trying to accomplish, if anything at all.[10] Mabel Dodge once wrote Eastman that "You frequently give me the impression of a lot of wild colts, getting a lot of fun out of kicking up their heels." Referring to their indictment under the Acts, she further notes "But I have never seen any reason for suppressing colts because they kick up their heels."[11]

The Masses was undoubtedly a collection of raucous individuals. The editorial "make-up" meetings were often riotous in themselves. Though the magazine came from the Left and many socialists worked for it, Dell writes that it "was not a socialist magazine but a magazine of free expression rather than a magazine devoted to any one political creed such as socialism . . . a magazine which would publish what they wished to express."[12]

That *The Masses* spent a great deal of time infuriating the public is no new statement, but the multitude of ways in which they did so is still fascinating. It might be their artwork; it might be their poems; it might have been their attitude. The magazine expressed topics considered taboo at the time, especially as many strove to cling on to so-called Victorian Era values: Free love, birth control, and a variety of social and political subjects guaranteed to annoy and appall the public.

Long before the American involvement in WWI the magazine faced suppression and lawsuits. Issues were kept from newsstands and library shelves, rejected by distribution companies, and once sued by the Associated Press for libel. Dell remembers that,

> From the point of view of some people in those days, the many of The
> Masses [sic] were all eligible for jail on several grounds. We were
> continually thumbing our noses at [then Secretary of the Society for the
> Suppression of Vice] Anthony Comstock and practically daring him to
> try and put us in jail on charges of obscenity (we were always printing
> pictures of naked women).[13]

Comstock at one point actually had a reason to pursue *The Masses* on defama-
tion charges. In a drawing by George Bellows, Comstock was portrayed as a
type of hairy shemale creature emerging from a shower. While the body
cannot be accounted for, the face and heavy presence of facial hair made it
impossible to ignore the point being made.[14]

Annoying mainstream society was especially easy with their ongoing feud
with the Associated Press (AP). As William O'Neill noted, this quarrel "did
much to establish the magazine's reputation, while at the same time demonstrating the lengths to which the editors were prepared to go in defense of its
freedom and flavor."[15] *Masses* cartoonist Art Young put a poignant, yet
humorous, touch on the situation with several drawings criticizing the mainstream press. He once likened their rivals to prostitutes; in another an AP
representative was poisoning a well labeled as "The News." The AP sued *The
Masses* for libel, but would quietly drop its suit. When this happened Young
rubbed it in their faces by recreating the News Well drawing by showing the
AP now adding "Truth" to the water.

These battles with mainstream society actually seemed amusing to
many, especially *The Masses* who thrived on the attention they were
getting. Many of its members were as sarcastic as Young, who was,
obviously, a very colorful character, others were far more serious

Max Eastman (1883–1969)

Eastman was a central focus of the trial of *The Masses*. A prolific writer and political activist, he had
already established a name for himself when he took the editor position of *The Masses*. Although he
faced indictment during the Acts, he created the magazine *The Liberator* along with his sister Crystal, a
journal that was more in line with Wilsonian policies. Born in Canandaigua, New York, earning a PhD in
Philosophy at Columbia University, he would become a central part of the Greenwich Village, New
York scene. He would later turn away from Socialism, especially after an almost 2-year tour of the
Soviet Union when he saw the power struggles between Josef Stalin and Leon Trotsky. This did not
mean he turned away from left-wing ideology completely, even translating some of Trotsky's works.
His personal ideologies would fluctuate throughout the years, even adopting some conservative
principles. He was portrayed in the 1981 Warren Beatty film *Reds*, which was about the life of fellow
radical John Reed.

Art Young (1866–1943)

Probably the most colorful character at *The Masses* trial, Young made a name for himself as an artist of Socialist cartoons, as well as a writer. Young was born in Illinois, and would attend numerous art schools, publishing his first cartoon in a Chicago newspaper *Nimble Nickel*. His politics would eventually evolve from more mainstream ideas to left wing, eventually identifying as a Socialist. Young believed in reforming social causes. Like O'Hare, he also ran for office on the Socialist ticket in New York in 1913; he was also unsuccessful. It was through his association with *The Masses* that his notoriety grew, especially his criticism of the mainstream media such as the Associated Press (who even sued Young once, but the suits were dropped). It was his work for *The Masses* that brought him under indictment. At issue was a drawing that the government claimed would obstruct enlistment. He slept quite a bit during both trials, with his outburst at the prosecuting attorney that ruined the latter's summation. Young continued to work, even joining *The Liberator* with Max Eastman. He died in 1943 in New York City.

in spreading radicalism and free thought. But it was this very reputation that mainstream society would be able to strike hard using the Acts.

As early as 1916 the Attorney General, the Department of Justice, and the Post Office collected complaints about *The Masses* using the mails for distributing their wares. In April 1917, several months before its troubles under the Acts, the magazine faced suppression by the Post Office. A drawing of a nude woman prompted the Postmaster of New York to write to Washington, DC asking for "advice as to the suitability of this issue in view of the picture of page 27."[16] William Lamarr, Solicitor of the United States, responded with a note barring it under "section four eighty regulations."[17] Business manager Merrill Rogers offered to remove the illustration for mailing purposes.

As mentioned, the American entry into WWI met with mixed reactions, and part of these reactions was fear of internal dissent. The wartime hysteria was already in full bloom by this time. The Acts only made it worse. Eastman remembers that this "elemental hysteria was whipped up by public officials and prominent citizens as well as the press. The country was advised to mob, whip, shoot and kill all dissenters."[18] Dell notes the "blind, blundering ferocity with which the government was undertaking to silence all minority opinion about the Espionage Act."[19] As Michael Kazin points out, "The U.S. declaration of war caused few American radicals to change their minds." In quoting Kate Richards O'Hare, one of the Acts' many victims, she said, "I am a socialist, a labor unionist and a believer in the Prince of Peace *first*, and an American second."[20]

When WWI broke out in 1914, *The Masses* joined in the cries that it was a vindication of Marxist theory. To those members adhering to Marxist thought, the imperialist powers at odds with each other was a fulfillment of prophecy. Untermeyer writes that, "War abroad united the editors of *The Masses* more

Kate Richards O'Hare (1876–1948)

Socialist O'Hare, prominent in the radical community, was well known for her oratorical skills, as well as contributing her editorial skills. Born Carrie Katherine Richards in Ottawa County, Kansas, her parents raised her and her siblings as Socialists almost immediately. In 1910 she tried to run for Congress in Kansas on the Socialist ticket; the attempt was unsuccessful. As her career grew, she worked in support of social causes. Her next attempt into politics was for Missouri senator, also on the Socialist ticket, in 1916. Again, this was a failure. While known for her speeches, what especially thrust her into the national limelight were her anti-war activities. Having joined the Socialist Party's Committee on War and Militarism, she made a speech in Bowman, North Dakota. O'Hare was sentenced to 5 years for her remarks and eventually sent to Missouri State Penitentiary in 1919. Due to an extensive movement, she was pardoned in 1920. However, she was a supporter of racial segregation. She continued to work for social and political causes until her death in California in 1948.

effectively than any local issue."[21] Their articles and drawings reflected disgust with the war, its implications, and effects. When the United States entered the conflict in 1917, they turned their focus from the international to the domestic. In 1949 Dell writes:

> The entrance of the United States into the war against Germany precipitated a crisis in the *Masses* affairs. We had been critical of the war from a socialist point of view, and we had given space to criticism of the war as such from a pacifist point of view. Some of our old contributors left us, new ones joined us, and we continued to criticize the war.[22]

After years of antagonizing their own kind, angering the public, and shocking the Puritans, *The Masses* found itself in serious trouble for violation of the Espionage Act. In July 1917, Merrill Rogers submitted the August 1917 issue of *The Masses* to George Creel, Chairman of the Committee of Public Information (noted by many to be the national censor), for an opinion regarding an advertisement. Rogers claims Creel said nothing in the magazine was objectionable. On July 5, 1917, the Postmaster of New York City, apparently ordered by Postmaster-General Albert Burleson, sent a note informing *The Masses* the issue was barred from the mails. When informed of the ban, the magazine offered to remove the offending passages. The Postmaster refused to furnish the information.

It was only after *The Masses* filed suit for an injunction did the Post Office identify the objectionable material. There were four cartoons; two by H.J. Glintenkamp condemning conscription and the loss of liberty (as depicted by a crumbling Liberty Bell); one by Boardman Robinson satirizing the Elihu Root mission to Petrograd; and one by Art Young referring to war profiteering by Wall Street. In addition, there were four articles cited; two by Eastman dealing with anarchists Emma Goldman and Alexander Berkman, and one addressing conscientious objectors; one unsigned, but attributed to Dell, also addressing conscientious objectors; and a poem by Josephine Bell, also referring to anarchists.

At the hearing, Judge Learned Hand, described by Eastman as "the most distinguished jurist in New York," granted the injunction.[23] Addressing the suppression of *The Masses* under the Espionage Act, Judge Hand felt "none of the language and none of the cartoons in this paper can be thought directly to counsel or advise insubordination or mutiny.[24] At least for the moment, *The Masses* emerged victorious.

The Post Office refused to admit defeat. While *The Masses* prepared its September issue, Judge Hough of Vermont granted a stay of execution on the injunction until the appeal could be heard. This meant the hearing would not take place until October, far too late to see the August issue.[25] To complicate matters, the Post Office refused to restore the mailing privileges on the pretext that, because *The Masses* did not mail the August issue they were not a regular periodical, and therefore undeserving of such rights. As Upton Sinclair writes, "Banning one issue from the mails and then taking away its mailing privilege for not publishing regularly was like a policeman knocking a man down and then when he cried with pain arresting him for disturbing the peace."[26]

The protests were in vain. On November 2, 1917, Judges Ward, Rogers, and Mayer of the Circuit Court of Appeals reversed the injunction, stating the courts would not overrule the Postmaster's actions "in a matter which involves his judgment and discretion, and which is within his jurisdiction."[27] Though denied use of the mails, *The Masses* managed to sell its issues on newsstands. Distribution was the least of their troubles. In October, 1917,

> the post office struck back through the Federal Government, and we were suddenly faced with an indictment on two counts: (1) that we had "conspired to effect insubordination or mutiny in the armed and naval forces of the United States" and (2) that we had "conspired" to obstruct enlistment and recruiting.[28]

In April, 1918, *The Masses* trial began. The defendants were Floyd Dell, Max Eastman, Merrill Rogers, Josephine Bell, and Art Young. Two of the others under indictment, John Reed and H.J. Glintenkamp, were not present. Glintenkamp fled to Mexico; Reed was in Moscow and unable to return for the trial. According to Granville Hicks, "Reed had left Russia with every intention of arriving in time."[29] As for Glintenkamp's cartoons, he once "used the Liberty Bell's cracks to suggest the fragility of wartime civil liberties, for publishing that image, the magazine editors would end up in court," although it was actually one of his other cartoons that would be used as evidence.[30] This would be the image of a skeleton measuring a prospective soldier for service.

Speaking for the defense was Morris Hillquit, famed socialist and unsuccessful candidate for various public offices in New York, and Dudley Field Malone, a former supporter of President Woodrow Wilson (Wilson appointed Malone Collector of the Port of New York, but Malone later resigned in disgust with Wilson over the treatment of women suffragists, one of whom was Malone's girlfriend). District Attorney Earl Barnes, along with two assistants, prosecuted the case. Presiding over the whole affair was Judge Augustus Hand, cousin of Learned Hand, the judge who earlier granted the injunction. According to Eastman, Hand was "a judge who could have upheld in a hurricane the dignity of the law."[31]

Jury selection became an arduous task for the defense. Hillquit hoped to select pacifist jurors, or at least those not members of any patriotic organizations. One juror admitted prejudice against socialism but would still weigh the evidence fairly.[32] Two separate accounts list the jury being filled solely with white-collar workers, "never a wage worker."[33] A band outside played patriotic songs. As Dell remembers, "Right now, American boys were getting killed on the battlefield, the band was playing patriotic airs outside the window, and it didn't look good for people who criticized the government."[34]

By the time of the trial, much changed with *The Masses*. To appease the Post Office it became *The Liberator*. Untermeyer claims "The aims of The Liberator were . . . less revolutionary."[35] Many of *The Liberator's* beliefs were very Wilsonian in nature, making the trial "anachronistic at best."[36] Hillquit immediately moved to quash the indictments. After hearing arguments, Judge Hand dismissed the first count, the conspiracy to incite mutiny in the armed forces, but the second count of conspiring to obstruct enlistment and recruitment remained. In his work on Reed, Hicks relates Reed's take on the whole situation, stating "All the ingenuity of the prosecution . . . had been devoted to an attempt to prove that the editors had quite literally conspired, had got together one day and said 'Go to, now, we will obstruct recruiting and enlistment to the injury of the service.'"[37]

The seriousness of the trial did not appear to the defendants, except for Eastman, Hillquit, and Malone. Untermeyer said they felt sorry for Hillquit and Malone, "who took it so seriously."[38] While the prosecution presented its case, the defendants treated the court to a comic display. Whenever the band outside played the *Star Spangled Banner*, Rogers, followed by the others, sprang to their feet in attention. Eastman remembers Judge Hand staring in bewilderment, eventually heaving "himself out of his chair," followed soon by the whole courtroom, "until the air played through." After this happened three more times, Judge Hand finally said "Well, I think we shall have to dispense with this ceremony from now on."[39]

Barnes placed 11 witnesses on the stand. According to Dell and Untermeyer, all Barnes did was prove "*The Masses* had been written, printed, sold, and circulated."[40] After the "patriotic" displays, and the prosecution's case, Hillquit moved to dismiss the remaining charges, citing lack of proof. Judge Hand denied the motion on the grounds that even though no evidence was provided to prove an actual conspiracy, "the fact of the defendants being associated with the same magazine constituted 'prima facie evidence' of conspiracy."[41] It was up to the jury to decide the rest.

The most unlikely of all the defendants was Josephine Bell. Until the trial, she had never met her "co-conspirators." After examining the poem causing her indictment, Judge Hand dismissed her case. Eastman said Judge Hand did so "with something between a sigh and a smile."[42]

The other defendants took the stand. Dell and Eastman performed with ease, not only citing their beliefs but avoiding verbal traps set by Barnes. Dell considered much of the trial as a game. Rogers' testimony rested on his presentation of the August issue to Creel (which must be noted as Creel was once a contributor to *The Masses*). Both at the trial and in the newspapers Creel denied giving approval, stating he thought the advertisement Rogers presented "epitomized treason."[43]

The real star of the trial was Art Young. His humor and easy-going style made him a lovable character. Of all the defendants, Young was probably the

Louise Bryant (1885–1936)

Although not a direct participant in any trials under the Acts, it was her involvement with John Reed that helped bring her name to the public eye. She was born in San Francisco as Anna Louise Mohan, eventually taking the surname of her stepfather. Bryant received an education. She was married when she met Reed, and, after becoming involved, moved to New York with Reed where she also became associated with the other staff members of *The Masses*. Although she and Reed married, they both had affairs outside of the union. They both traveled to Russia to see the revolution, and burgeoning Soviet system, growing. Bryant made a name for herself writing articles for the Hearst newspapers, although Reed was still the better known writer. When Reed died in 1920, Bryant continued her own writing, and remarried. Reed's book *Ten Days that Shook the World* still remains a classic, but Bryant's own account *Six Red Months in Russia* (1918) is equally as important. She supported the Bolshevik cause, and even appeared before a Senate subcommittee to discuss Bolshevism. The 1981 films *Reds* depicts the life she shared with Reed. She drank heavily after Reed's death, eventually dying of a brain hemorrhage in 1936. An overlooked radical, her participation in the movement was unique for a woman at the time.

most relaxed. In fact, he was so relaxed he slept through a good portion of the trial. Just after the charges against Bell were dropped, "the rest breathed more lightly—all except Art Young, who was breathing far more heavily. He was asleep."[44] Dell recalls "Barnes said that it almost made him cry to have to ask the jury to send Art Young to prison."[45]

The defense summation questioned the charges, the evidence, and argued for the right to freedom of opinion. Dell believes Barnes' summation "tried to persuade the jury that they could only prove their patriotism by sending us to prison."[46] Eastman felt that though Barnes seemed convinced they were guilty and should go to prison, as with Art Young, he "seemed reluctant to send us there."[47]

Before sending the jury out to deliberate, Judge Hand reminded the jury of the right to free speech and opinion.[48] The deliberation itself, however, was lengthy; the jury often returned to request additional instructions. After three days, the jury announced it was hopelessly deadlocked. Judge Hand declared a mistrial and released the defendants. After 9 days of trial and 3 of deliberation, the defendants felt the whole affair was over. It was not to be. Over the opposition of Hillquit and Malone, the prosecution moved to try *The Masses* again.

The second trial took place in June, 1918. Hillquit and Malone were not available as defense attorneys, having other commitments. Seymour Stedman, attorney for labor leader and socialist Eugene Debs, traveled to New York to assist them (Debs' conviction under the Acts was just one month earlier and will be discussed below). Stedman's health mostly kept him from the courtroom, leaving the defense up to Charles Recht. The other changes were Martin J. Manton as the presiding judge, and the presence of John Reed, returned from Russia. Reed's presence was welcomed. As mentioned earlier, he desired to be present for the first trial. The mistrial and release of his co-defendants occurred a mere one day before his arrival back into the country. Outside of the defendants (without, of course, Josephine Bell), the one returning participant was that Earl Barnes was again the prosecutor.

By the time of the second trial the war was over and the defendants, as noted above, supported many of Wilson's policies. Nevertheless, the trial proceeded with much of the same atmosphere as the first, including the band outside. The jury selection was similar to the first. Several accounts describe one juror listing his business as "Wall Street," admitting his prejudice against socialism. "I don't know what it is, but I'm opposed to it."[49] Some of the defendants were convinced they would not be as lucky the second time. "We had criticized the government in wartime, and that was conspiracy enough."[50]

Many of the speeches made in the first trial were made in the second. Reed spoke of his experiences as a war correspondent in Mexico and Europe. Eastman's speech packed the courtroom with people "from other

John Reed (1887–1920)

Probably the most famous of all those of *The Masses* indicted under the Acts, Reed was a journalist and poet whose work *Ten Days that Shook the World* was his eyewitness account of the 1917 Bolshevik revolution. Reed was born in Portland, Oregon, and was educated at Harvard College, where he was very active in many school activities. Determined to be a journalist, he became part of the Bohemian scene in Greenwich Village. He would join *The Masses*, contributing many articles. He would witness many events of the Mexican revolution, which culminated in his book *Insurgent Mexico*. When WWI broke out, Reed immediately opposed the conflict. Reed supported Wilson's re-election, especially on the proposition the U.S. would not enter the war. He was able to sail to Russia where he witnessed many of the events written about in the *Ten Days* book, although some doubt he actually saw some of these occurrences. He was not present for the first *Masses* trial but was present for the second. Eventually the Socialist Part split into different factions, of which Reed was part of the creation of the Communist Labor Party of America (CLP), and went back to Russia to seek recognition. After a series of events whereby he was arrested, he made it to Moscow. While he desired to return to the U.S., typhoid struck and killed him. He was the only American buried in the Kremlin Wall. He was immortalized in the 1981 Warren Beatty film *Reds*.

parts of the building."[51] Dell restated his positions. Young displayed his irritation with having to explain his artwork.

The time came for Barnes to sum up his arguments. The description of Barnes' oration place him as mustering up every ounce of patriotism he could find, "wrapping himself in the flag" in hopes of winning a conviction: "Somewhere in France a man lies dead. He is but one of a thousand whose voices are now silent. He died for you and he died for me. He died for Max Eastman. He died for John Reed. He died for Merrill Rogers. He demands that these men be punished." It was at this point that Young awoke from his customary slumber and said "What! Didn't he die for me too?" Untermeyer contends this was done in a loud voice while Eastman said it was a loud whisper. Regardless of how it was said, Young's exclamation was enough to ruin the entire speech, and possibly contributed to yet another hung jury.[52]

Judge Manton's charge to the jury was similar to Hand's. After five days of trial, the jury needed only Friday afternoon and part of Saturday to announce another disagreement. Whereas the first jury had only one member in favor of acquittal, the second was far more favorable with eight. The case was dropped, impounded materials returned, and the defendants went back to work on *The Liberator*, from which Reed would resign as editor but remain as a contributor.

The prominence of *The Masses* made one newspaper refer to the case as "What may be the most important test case in America of free press in war time."[53] A letter dated May 1, 1918, from Walter Nelles to Morris Hillquit notes that "Such inconsistencies [in Espionage Act cases] point the need for an authoritative ruling."[54] Hillquit defended others indicted under the Espionage Act. He obviously attempted to establish this ruling himself. If the government won a conviction against *The Masses*, it is possible future decisions might have been easier. The divided juries simply reflected the divided sentiments in America.

But *The Masses* had a notoriety that would, and could, be either a blessing or a curse. Clowning around in court may have amused some while irritating others, there were those convicted under the Acts who would not enjoy such a "privilege." Some of these people had names as familiar as *The Masses*, but for different reasons. Four of such individuals indicted and/or convicted under the Acts are Scott Nearing, Mollie Steimer, Kate Richards O'Hare, and Eugene Debs (Nearing and Debs will be discussed in Chapter 4). One person who was ostracized merely for opposing the war was the infamous Progressive reformer Jane Addams. But there were many others who felt the grip of the Acts, and for the most harmless of reasons.

But intriguing questions remained: What was an activity that truly threatened the war effort and put American lives at risk? What was merely an exercise of free speech voicing one's own opinions? What was simply reporting the horrors of war? The line was quite blurred. At times the line was very defined since many left wing radicals (among others) felt the country's entrance into the war was merely for economic interests.

Historians such as Donalson, Thomas Fleming, and Paul L. Murphy have recounted numerous indictments and actions against alleged dissenters.[55] As Fleming mentions, "At first, some judges dismissed charges

Jane Addams (1860–1935)

Addams will always be remembered as arguably the greatest female reformer of the Progressive Era. Although she worked tirelessly to make the country, and the world, a better place, her anti-war stance made her the target of those who supported the suppression of dissents. Addams was born in Cedarville, Illinois. She suffered from a lifetime of health problems due to having contracted tuberculosis of the spine as a child. She was well educated, and was enamored by the idea of establishing a settlement house where people could better themselves by exposure to cultural pursuits and practical training. Her infamous Hull House in Chicago is still a major part of both Chicago and national history. In 1915 she joined the Women's Peace Party, eventually becoming its chairperson. Being a pacifist, she strongly opposed WWI, and was thus vilified nationally. Despite many speeches opposing the war, she was never indicted under the Acts. In 1931, well after WWI, she became the first woman to win the Nobel Peace Prize, and the very people who criticized her anti-war activities were the first to applaud her prize. She died in Chicago, the very town she especially helped to improve.

against men and women who distributed literature or spoke out against the draft. Popular among protesters was the pamphlet *The Price We Pay*, which described the war in France in horrific terms." One man was actually convicted under the infamous phrase "clear and present danger doctrine" since part of the pamphlet denounced the supposed economic reasons for going to war.[56] But, as Geoffrey Stone sees it, as the war raged on, most "judges during the war were determined to impose severe sentences on those charged with disloyalty, and no details of legislative interpretation or appeals to the first amendment would stand in the way."[57]

In a seemingly bizarre twist of prosecution under the Espionage Act, the 1917 film *Spirit of '76* found itself at the center of controversy. Produced by Robert Goldstein and directed by Frank Montgomery, the film was a depiction of the American Revolution, and released just after the U.S. entry into the war. The film showed numerous scenes of British cruelty and sexual situations, although many of the scenes were fictitious and had absolutely no factual basis. One such alleged scene was a British soldier impaling a baby with a bayonet.

Still, when the film was going to be shown in Chicago, the print was confiscated. Goldstein went to court over the seizure and offered to remove the offending scenes, and the film was thus shown. But, some months later, the film was shown in Los Angeles with the scenes restored, and Goldstein was arrested. At that time movies were not considered protected under the First Amendment, and, using the Espionage Act, "the judge found Goldstein guilty of exhibiting 'exaggerated scenes of British cruelty,' which might make people 'question the good faith of our ally, Great Britain.'"[58] Goldstein was sentenced to 10 years in prison, which Wilson later reduced to 3 years. No prints of the film are known to exist.[59]

Prosecution of the Acts knew no gender boundaries, nor did anyone who wished to criticize dissenters. As noted above, three women who especially achieved notoriety during this time were Mollie Steimer, Kate Richards O'Hare, and Jane Addams. While only Steimer and O'Hare were prosecuted, Addams endured intense criticism that lasted for years.

Steimer was born in Russia in 1897, immigrating to the United States while a teenager, winding up in New York City. Like so many other countless immigrants, and typical of many teenage laborers, she went to work in the garment industry. And, as so many factory workers were wont to do, Steimer became part of the trade labor union movement. She also became influenced by left wing ideology, especially Anarchy. She would later become friends with noted Anarchist Emma Goldman, another female Russian immigrant who the government would consider to be an enemy of the state.

Steimer fell in with a group of other Anarchists. Like her fellow Anarchists, along with Socialists and Communists, they were opposed to the war and its capitalistic nature. They tried to quietly distribute an anti-war tract called *Frayhayt*, a word that meant "freedom." Besides denouncing the war and promoting resistance to the draft, it also promoted Anarchist revolutionary ideology. However, after one of the tracts was tossed into the streets of New York City, Steimer was arrested on August 23, 1918.

Along with three others, Steimer was convicted under the Espionage Act, and sentenced to 15 years in prison (her co-defendants each received 20 years). Steimer never once waivered in her devotion to Anarchy. She was released on bail, but the U.S. Supreme Court was considering other cases under the Espionage Act (See Chapter 4), and she continued to be arrested, although never charged with additional counts. Due to the Supreme Court upholding the validity of the Acts, she was eventually sent to prison. In 1922, she was deported back to Russia.[60]

Kate Richards O'Hare was another especially colorful character in the radical sector. As Michael Kazin writes, O'Hare was "an engaging orator from the Great Plains, revealed that Christianity remained vital to her part of the left: 'I am a socialist, a labor unionist and a believer in the Prince of Peace *first*, and an American second.'"[61] Despite her profession to Christianity, her other self-imposed labels would not do her any favors during WWI.

Born in Kansas in 1876, she was raised by her parents to believe in Socialism. She ran for public office twice on the Socialist ticket; the first in 1910 for the U.S. Congress, then again in 1916 for the U.S. Senate. While both efforts ended in defeat, her reputation as an orator and working tirelessly to promote the labor movement won her many admirers.

As with Steimer, and so many others, she opposed WWI. It was in 1917 in North Dakota that she delivered an anti-war speech. In a pattern repeated by so many others, she was arrested under the Espionage Act. She was convicted, and sent to a Missouri prison in 1919. Although so many others met a similar fate, O'Hare had the benefit of many supporters who rallied to her cause. She was pardoned in 1920.[62]

The one person who was vilified during the war, but never prosecuted, was the noted Progressive Jane Addams. Known so well as a Progressive championing the rights of women, children, and the downtrodden, Addams didn't just help others improve their lives, she encouraged them to take charge as well. Besides activism, she also provided educational programs.

Long known as an anti-war activist and pacifist, she opposed the U.S. annexation of the Philippines. When WWI broke out, she worked with several groups who promoted a peaceful solution to the conflict. Addams' criticism of war did not abate when the U.S. entered the conflict. This was met with scorn from many segments of society. She was denounced by newspapers. Interestingly enough, although many labeled her as unpatriotic, just like the radical left, she was not prosecuted for her anti-war stance. In 1931 she became the first woman to win the Nobel Peace prize. Those who vilified her in the past were often the first to applaud such a momentous achievement.[63]

While it is easy to portray those prosecuted and/or criticized during the WWI era, it is not always easy for some to acknowledge who supported such actions. As noted previously, the Acts had more supporters than some wish to admit. The easiest place to start is within the federal government. And the easiest person to discuss first is Burleson.

Burleson's part in the prosecution of *The Masses* has already been noted. He suppressed the magazine from the mails, although it could still be sold on newsstands, which was beyond his immediate control. Although many of his original policies strove to improve the U.S. postal service, his image as an extreme reactionary will remain foremost in American memory (see p.51 for biographical information).

Burleson was appointed in March, 1913, by Wilson. Even before the U.S. entry into WWI, Burleson used his office to forbid any type of mail from countries involved in the conflict, although the focus, of course, was on anything from Germany. With the passage of the Espionage Act, in retrospect, it seems Burleson was given carte blanche to go after anyone who displeased him.

Burleson saw the Espionage Act as a way to further his own personal agenda. As Nancy Gentile Ford writes, "Throughout the war, it became clear that Burleson, an anti-radical superpatriot—'the foremost official enemy of dissidents'—continually overstepped his authority in a personal crusade for conformity."[64] Post Office workers were told to be on the lookout for any potential subversive mailings. To many, this need for conformity was also racial, as Burleson also previously succeeded in the racial segregation of the Post Office.

Besides using the legal power of the Espionage Act to suppress dissent, Burleson used his powers in economic ways. The one way he went against radical publications, like *The Masses*, was by curtailing their mailing privileges. The best way to do so was through the postage rates. Besides outright objection to material in the mailings, Burleson used "the restriction of second-class-mail privileges. The latter could bankrupt a press that could not afford the expense of first-class mass mailings."[65]

As noted earlier, the federal government passed legislation regulating communications between the warring European nations. Burleson would argue, and some would agree with him, that seemingly harmless letters might contain information harmful to the country. But, "Burleson also overstepped his authority by cutting off second-class-mailing privileges of many ethnic presses without cause."[66] Even without Burleson's participation, any seemingly bad presence could easily be brought to his attention by post office workers.

One of the most interesting people involved in all of the prosecutions under the Acts is George Creel. Born in 1876, he was very attached to his mother, although once he ran away from home at the age of 15, staying away a year. He would fall into the newspaper business, even once served as a police commissioner in Denver. He worked for Wilson's re-election, using his journalist background to help.

On April 14, 1917, Wilson established by executive order the Committee on Public Information (CPI), with Creel at the helm. As noted above with the case of *The Masses*, he was considered to be the national censor. The CPI also included cabinet members of the Secretaries of State, War, and Navy. The point was to unite American public opinion by utilizing publicity, through pamphlets, news releases, posters, movies, and volunteer speakers. CPI's budget was set at $100 million, something that many members of Congress did not like as there was no accounting for any spending, and was "viewing Creel's committee as a Wilson publicity machine."[67]

By utilizing a variety of people from many fields, the CPI "enthusiastically presented the war as an emotional crusade and painted anyone who did not support the cause as a danger to America."[68] Recent immigrants were a favorite audience for telling them to prove their patriotism. Their volunteer speakers—at 75,000—were called the "Four Minute Men" for their brief, but hopefully effective, efforts to promote the war effort. When the war ended, so did the CPI.

If there was any group who one could say enjoyed this period it was the American Protective League (APL). As Goldstein relates,

> the official purpose of the APL, which numbered three hundred fifty thousand person by the end of the war in over six hundred cities [although some claim the number was two hundred fifty thousand] was to help the government with such matters as food rationing and putting the conscription machinery into operation, along with specific intelligence operations such as investigating the loyalty of soldiers and government personnel and . . . investigating the loyalty of Americans who wished to leave the country for any reason.[69]

But the true extent of the APL's powers was not specifically defined.

The APL was created in 1917 by A.M. Briggs. Like other ultra-patriots, Briggs did not think government agencies were going far enough to protect the country against potential enemies. Attorney General Thomas Watt Gregory gave his approval. Many members of the APL wore badges reading "American Protective League—Secret Service."

While working with the Justice Department, the APL participated in activities that many considered illegal, and rightfully so. Composed of

American Protective League (APL)

A group active during the WWI years, the APL was a private organization that went after anyone of German descent who they perceived to be a threat to the country and the war effort. Besides anyone with German blood who might be in sympathy with Germany, the APL also targeted anyone in the radical community who might work against the war effort, and this included pacifists. Created by Chicago businessman A.M. Briggs, the APL accused the federal government of not going far enough to counter anti-war activities. Given the blessing from the Department of Justice, the APL began operations in 1917. They portrayed themselves as agents of the federal government, even wearing badges advertising to this effect. Besides pursuing supposed dissenters, the APL also carried on extensive spying activities, and conducted raids. Those who appeared to be violating rationing regulations were suspect. While the exact membership numbers are in dispute, it is said the APL had anywhere from 250,000 to 350,000 members. There was considerable backlash against the APL, and other such private groups who preyed on citizens. However, when the war was over, their relevance greatly diminished. A. Mitchell Palmer, who assumed the post of Attorney General, refused to work with the APL. The group was eventually dissolved, although some of its members continued such activities for years.

"upper social, economic and political crust of each community," they participated in a variety of actions against anyone they felt was a threat.[70] They spied on people through planted operatives, wiretapping, and opening mail. Although they did not specifically have the authority, they participated in arrests, and even in the outright harassment—physical and otherwise—of suspected individuals. With the Justice Department, across the country they joined in raids whereby thousands were arrested under the flimsiest of reasons. It wasn't until 1919 that the APL was being roped in by the new Attorney A. Mitchell Palmer, who was refusing to work with them. As with the CPI, with the end of the war came the end of the organization.

U.S. Attorney General Thomas Watt Gregory had a little more difficult time. Before the American involvement in WWI, as mentioned, there was fear of foreign spies. The fear of Germans inciting Irish and Indians into insurrection against their colonizers Great Britain, but there were British agents at work as well. Despite the cries for action, Gregory

maintained that the Justice Department could take no action because the agents were not violating federal law. The courts had held that the treason statute covered all those "owing allegiance to the United States," including foreigners domiciled in the United States; but activities of spies and saboteurs in peacetime did not come under the definition of treason—waging war or give aid and comfort to the enemy.[71]

Gregory pleaded to the federal government to pass the necessary legislation, holding that "his Bureau of Investigation [later the Federal Bureau of Investigation, or FBI] agents had no legal right to investigate activities that were not in violation of federal law."[72] He also knew that many agents were acting on their own and without proper authority. Furthermore, Gregory believed that until a federal law was in place, the states should do such prosecution.

With the Acts, the federal government was now officially persecuting and prosecuting dissenters of any sort. Private groups and individuals jumped on the bandwagon. Trouble was once again brewing in Russia, and there was fear that the country might pull out of the war since they were not only losing the war in the most embarrassing fashion, but the radical sector there was making waves.

When Russia shocked the world with its two revolutions in 1917, the fear of radicalism in the United States grew even more. The first revolution in March removed the Romanov dynasty. The country went through several provisional governments before the Bolsheviks staged their own revolution in November. While it would take several years for the Bolsheviks, led by Vladimir Lenin, to firmly establish control, Russia was effectively pulled from the war.

Conducting the war now took a whole new turn.

NOTES

1 Daniel G. Donalson, *The Espionage and Sedition Acts of World War I: Using Wartime Loyalty Laws for Revenge and Profit* (El Paso, TX: LFB Scholarly Publishing, 2012), 1.

2 Christopher Capozzola, *Uncle Sam Wants You: World War I and the Making of the Modern American Citizen* (Oxford, UK: Oxford University Press, 2008), 150.

3 Elizabeth Stevenson, *Babbitts and Bohemians: The American 1920s* (New York: Macmillan Company, 1967), 38.

4 Robert Justin Goldstein, *Political Repression in Modern America: 1870 to the Present* (Cambridge: Schenkman, 1978), 113.

5 Leslie Fishbein, *Rebels in Bohemia* (Chapel Hill, NC: The University of North Carolina Press, 1982).

6 John E. Hart, *Floyd Dell* (New York: Twayne, 1971), 55.

7 Louis Untermeyer, *From Another World* (New York: Harcourt Brace, 1939), 42.

8 Max Eastman, "Floyd Dell in the Nick of Time," Floyd Dell Papers.

9 Ibid.

10 John Diggins, *The American Left in the Twentieth Century* (New York: Harcourt Brace Jovanovich, 1973), 80.

11 Mabel Dodge, Letter to Max Eastman, no precise date available, Floyd Dell Papers.

12   Dell, "Review of Max Eastman's 'Enjoyment of Living,'" Handwritten copy, Floyd Dell Papers.
13   Floyd Dell, "Memories of the Old Masses," *American Mercury* 68 (April 1949), 485.
14   William O'Neill, Ed., *Echoes of Revolt: The Masses 1911–1917* (Chicago, IL: Ivan R. Dee, 1966), 45.
15   Ibid., 33.
16   Post Office Department Records, 6 April 1917, Box 16, Folder 46578, Record Group 28, National Archives, Washington, D.C.
17   Ibid., 7 April 1917.
18   Max Eastman, *Love and Revolution* (New York: Random House, 1964), 29.
19   Dell, "Memories of the Old Masses," 486.
20   Michael Kazin, *American Dreamers: How the Left Changed a Nation* (New York: Alfred A. Knopf, 2011), 147.
21   Untermeyer, 64.
22   Dell, "Memories of the Old Masses," 486.
23   Eastman, 59–60; Zechariah Chafee, Free Speech in the United States (Cambridge, MA: Harvard University Press, 1948).
24   *Masses Publishing Co. v. Patten*, 244 Federal Reporter, 540–541, District Court, S.D. New York, 24 July 1917.
25   Eastman, 61.
26   As quoted in H.C. Peterson and Gilbert C. Fite, *Opponents of War* (Madison, WI: University of Wisconsin Press, 1957), 93.
27   *Masses Publishing Co. v. Patten*, 246 Federal Reporter, 38–39, Circuit Court of Appeals, Second Circuit, 2 November 1917.
28   Untermeyer, 67.
29   Greenville Hicks, *John Reed: The Making of a Revolutionary* (New York: Benjamin Blom, 1968), 304.
30   Capozzola, 144.
31   Eastman, 85.
32   "Max Eastman Trial Starts," *Evening Globe*, New York City, 15 April 1918, reproduced from the Morris Hillquit Papers (microfilmed—hereinafter Hillquit Papers), Reel 8, No. 1056, State Historical Society of Wisconsin.
33   Unidentifiable newspaper article, 1918, Hillquit Papers, Reel 8; Dell, "The Story of the Trial," *The Liberator* (June 1918): 8.
34   Dell, "Memories of the Old Masses," 486.
35   Untermeyer, 76.
36   Fishbein, 25.
37   Hicks, 304.
38   Untermeyer, 69.
39   Eastman, 86.
40   Untermeyer, 69; Dell, *Homecoming: An Autobiography* (New York: Farrar & Rinehart, 1933), 314–315.
41   Dell, "The Story of the Trial," 8.
42   Eastman, 92.
43   Eastman, 89; "Creel Denies He OK'd Pledge," *Times*, New York City, 25 April 1918, reproduced from Hillquit Papers, Reel 8. Eastman claims Creel's testimony "differed so little from what Merrill had said that it made no real point for the

prosecution." However, Creel's testimony did differ from Rogers' on the very point of approval of the August 1917, issue of *The Masses*.

44 Untermeyer, 70.
45 Dell, "Memories of the Old Masses," 486.
46 Dell, "The Story of the Trial," 17.
47 Eastman, 97.
48 *Evening Call*, New York City, 26 April 1918, reproduced from Hillquit Papers, Reel 8.
49 Untermeyer, 74.
50 Dell, "Memories of the Old Masses," 486.
51 Eastman, 121.
52 Untermeyer, 76; Eastman, 122.
53 Unidentifiable newspaper article, 16 April 1918, reproduced from Morris Hillquit Papers, Reel 8.
54 Walter Nelles, letter to Morris Hillquit, 1 May 1918, Reel 2, Morris Hillquit Papers.
55 See Donalson; Paul L. Murphy, *World War I and the Origin of Civil Liberties in the United States* (New York: W.W. Norton, 1979); and Thomas Fleming, *The Illusion of Victory* (New York: Basic Books, 2003).
56 Fleming, 107. Fleming also relates the lynch mob mentality against various groups as Donalson also describes. This particular case will be discussed below.
57 Geoffrey R. Stone, *Perilous Times: Free Speech in Wartime* (New York: W.W. Norton, 2005), 170.
58 Fleming, 190.
59 See also Anthony Slide, *Robert Goldstein and 'The Spirit of '76'* (New York: Scarecrow Press, 1993).
60 For additional information on Mollie Steimer, see Paul Avrich, *Anarchist Portraits* (Princeton, CT: Princeton University Press, 1988); and Kathleen Kennedy, *Disloyal Mothers and Scurrilous Citizens: Women and Subversion during World War I* (Bloomington, IN: Indiana University Press, 1999).
61 Kazin, 147.
62 See Kate Richards O'Hare, *In Prison* (Seattle, WI: University of Washington Press, reprint 1976); Neil K. Basen, "Kate Richards O'Hare: The 'First Lady' of American Socialism, 1910–1917," *Labor History* 21 (Spring 1980): 165–199; Philip S. Foner and Sally M. Miller, Eds., *Kate Richards O'Hare: Selected Writings and Speeches* (Baton Rouge, LA: Louisiana State University Press, 1982); and Sally M. Miller, *From Prairie to Prison: The Life of Socialist Activist Kate Richards O'Hare* (Columbia, MO: University of Missouri Press, 1993).
63 See Louise W. Knight, *Jane Addams: Spirit in Action* (New York: W.W. Norton, 2010); and Allen F. Davis, *American Heroine: The Life and Legend of Jane Addams* (Lanham, MD: Ivan R. Dee, 2000).
64 Nancy Gentile Ford, *Issues of War and Peace* (Westport, CT: Greenwood Press, 2002), 183.
65 Ibid.
66 Ibid., 164.
67 Fleming, 97
68 Ford, 181.
69 Goldstein, 111.
70 Ibid.

71 Joan M. Jensen, *The Price of Vigilance* (Chicago, IL: Rand McNally, 1968), 10.
72 Ibid., 12

BIBLIOGRAPHY

Avrich, Paul. *Anarchist Portraits*. Princeton, CT: Princeton University Press, 1988.
Basen, Neil K. "Kate Richards O'Hare: The 'First Lady' of American Socialism, 1910–1917." *Labor History* 21 (Spring 1980): 165–199.
Capozzola, Christopher. *Uncle Sam Wants You: World War I and the Making of the Modern American Citizen*. Oxford, UK: Oxford University Press, 2008.
Davis, Allen F. *American Heroine: The Life and Legend of Jane Addams*. Lanham, MD: Ivan R. Dee, 2000.
Dell, Floyd. "Memories of the Old Masses," *American Mercury* 68 (April 1949).
———. *Homecoming: An Autobiography*. New York: Farrar & Rinehart, 1933.
Diggins, John. *The American Left in the Twentieth Century*. New York: Harcourt Brace Jovanovich, 1973.
Donalson, Daniel G. *The Espionage and Sedition Acts of World War I: Using Wartime Loyalty Laws for Revenge and Profit*. El Paso, TX: LFB Scholarly Publishing, 2012.
Eastman, Max. *Love and Revolution*. New York: Random House, 1964.
Fishbein, Leslie. *Rebels in Bohemia*. Chapel Hill, NC: The University of North Carolina Press, 1982.
Fleming, Thomas. *The Illusion of Victory*. New York: Basic Books, 2003.
Floyd Dell Papers. Newberry Library, Chicago, IL.
Foner, Philip S. and Sally M. Miller, Eds. *Kate Richards O'Hare: Selected Writings and Speeches*. Baton Rouge, LA: Louisiana State University Press, 1982.
Ford, Nancy Gentile. *Issues of War and Peace*. Westport, CT: Greenwood Press, 2002.
Goldstein, Robert Justin. *Political Repression in Modern America: 1870 to the Present*. Cambridge, MA: Schenkman, 1978.
Hart, John E. *Floyd Dell*. New York: Twayne, 1971.
Hicks, Greenville. *John Reed: The Making of a Revolutionary*. New York: Benjamin Blom, 1968.
Jensen, Joan M. *The Price of Vigilance*. Chicago, IL: Rand McNally, 1968.
Kazin, Michael. *American Dreamers: How the Left Changed a Nation*. New York: Alfred A. Knopf, 2011.
Kennedy, Kathleen. *Disloyal Mothers and Scurrilous Citizens: Women and Subversion during World War I*. Bloomington, IN: Indiana University Press, 1999.
Knight, Louise. *Jane Addams: Spirit in Action*. New York: W.W. Norton, 2010.
Masses Publishing Co. v. Patten, 244 Federal Reporter, 540–541, District Court, S.D. New York, 24 July 1917.
Masses Publishing Co. v. Patten, 246 Federal Reporter, 38–39, Circuit Court of Appeals, Second Circuit, 2 November 1917.
Miller, Sally M. *From Prairie to Prison: The Life of Socialist Activist Kate Richards O'Hare*. Columbia, MO: University of Missouri Press, 1993.
Morris Hillquit Papers. Library of Congress, Washington, D.C.
Murphy, Paul L. *World War I and the Origin of Civil Liberties in the United States*. New York: W.W. Norton, 1979.

O'Hare, Kate Richards. *In Prison*. Seattle, WA: University of Washington Press, reprint 1976.

O'Neill, William, Ed., *Echoes of Revolt: The Masses 1911–1917*. Chicago, IL: Ivan R. Dee, 1966.

Peterson, H.C. and C. Gilbert Fite, *Opponents of War*. Madison, WI: University of Wisconsin Press, 1957.

Post Office Department Records. National Archives, Washington, D.C.

Slide, Anthony. *Robert Goldstein and "The Spirit of '76."* New York: Scarecrow Press, 1993.

Stevenson, Elizabeth. *Babbitts and Bohemians: The American 1920s*. New York: Macmillan Company, 1967.

Stone, Geoffrey R. *Perilous Times: Free Speech in Wartime*. New York: W.W. Norton, 2005.

Untermeyer, Louis. *From Another World*. New York: Harcourt Brace, 1939.

CHAPTER 4

America Reacts

In a letter from Woodrow Wilson to Postmaster Albert S. Burleson on October 11, 1917, the President writes "I am sure you will agree with me that we must act with the utmost caution and liberality in all our censorship," keeping their actions with at least the moderates, "the very sort of people whose judgment we would like to approve of what we do."[1] Burleson responded by saying "I emphatically dissent from the insinuation . . . that there has been ruthless enforcement of the Espionage Act. In the discharge of my duty under this law the weak and the strong, the poor and the rich have been accorded like treatment."[2] Nothing could have been further from the truth.

However, Wilson's letter meant little to Burleson. George P. West interviewed Burleson in the November 21, 1917, edition of the *New York Post*. In this article, West defended Max Eastman as "open and sincere," who in fact endorsed Wilson's policies. Burleson responded by saying "I regard Max Eastman as no better than a traitor, and the stuff he has been printing as rank treason . . . Traitors all look alike to me, I don't care whether they are

---

Albert Sydney Burleson (1863–1937)

Burleson is best remembered as the United States Postmaster General under the Wilson administration, and for his actions during WWI in using the Acts to suppress mailing privileges of any materials suspected of violating the Acts. He is also remembered for segregating the U.S. Post Office, even firing black workers. He was born in San Marcos, Texas, and was appointed Postmaster General in 1913. In 1915, even before the U.S. entry into the war and the passage of the Acts, he barred mailings coming from any of the European countries at war. He highly supported the Espionage Act, and directed all postmasters to report suspicious mailings. Under his leadership, the Post Office directed the telephone and telegraph services, a cause he supported until his death in 1937.

sincere or not." He continued by saying "What these editors want is a chance to spew out all their poison and do all the mischief they are capable of before we can reach them. They won't succeed."[3]

Burleson's prejudice is evidenced in another situation in 1919. He confronted the *Washington Post* over an article entitled "Hun Hisses Wilson." Though the war was over, the Espionage Act still in force, and prosecutions still in court, Burleson by-passed the chance to press charges against the paper for printing an article considered to be a personal attack on the postal authorities.

> I acquit the editorial management of the *Post* of responsibility for this article, but it is distressing when one thinks that in any newspaper making even a pretense of decent fairness, such a dastardly attempt as this to besmirch a governmental establishment could be made.[4]

Burleson's commitment to "fair treatment" seemed to have been lost.

Before the obligatory examination of the U.S. Supreme Court cases dealing with the Acts, it is imperative to discuss some of the lesser known cases. Nearing is another interesting character during the time. While his situation may not receive as much attention as the Supreme Court cases, it is nevertheless vital to discuss.

Nearing was born in Pennsylvania in 1883. As opposed to others who joined the radical movement, Nearing actually grew up in a privileged atmosphere, but this did not stop him from realizing the inequalities in society. A well-educated man, Nearing still developed a social conscious. His policies cost him a job at the University of Pennsylvania, although he would continue teaching at Toledo University, another job he would lose. His reputation as

Scott Nearing (1883–1983)

Nearing's trial under the Acts is one of the most famous. Known for his radical ideas, he was also established as a writer and an economist. While he was luckier than most, his trial was noted across the country. He was born in Morris Run, Pennsylvania into somewhat a form of privilege. He would attend the Wharton School of Business, which had a profound influence on him. He was also becoming more and more of a social activist, something that would cost him a teaching job at Wharton and catching the eye of the nation's radical movement. He would later lose a job at Toledo University due to his anti-war sentiments. He landed in New York where he delivered a series of speeches, but it was his pamphlet *The Great Madness* that earned him an indictment under the Espionage Act. He was acquitted, and later spent a few months in the Soviet Union and China. Nearing also opposed World War II. He continued to write, and be controversial up to his death.

radical earned him a great deal of attention across the country, especially as he joined the Socialist Party.

Along with the American Socialist Society (ASS), and through the Rand School of Social Sciences, Nearing published *The Great Madness: A Victory for the American Plutocracy*. Two indictments came down in 1918, one on March 21 and the other on May 13. As John Saltmarsh writes, "In sum, they charged that Nearing and the ASS had in writing *The Great Madness* separately violated, and together conspired to violate, Section 3 of the Espionage Act and the Selective Service Act."[5]

Nearing's friends quickly came to his defense, and motions were made to quash the indictments. Acting on Nearing's defense was none other than Morris Hillquit, who defended *The Masses* in the first trial (See Chapter 3). Even members of the prosecution felt the case was weak, as the tract was more about plutocracy than the war.[6] Hillquit's legal motions resulted in the second indictment noted above.

In a case involving some similar faces, a decision about the charges took an interesting turn. The charge Judge Augustus Hand gave to the jury in the first *Masses* trial differed from his cousin Learned's ruling concerning the case *United States v. Nearing*. The former reminded the jury of a citizen's right to unintentionally obstruct the enlistment process due to disapproval of war and conscription; the latter ruled "To persuade or advise or counsel eligible persons not to volunteer certainly obstructs the purpose of that service, whether the effort be successful or not."[7] While Hand dismissed two counts, he allowed the others to stand.

The actual trial was in February, 1919, months after the end of hostilities. Nearing never ceased expressing his anti-war feelings, and was monitored by government agents looking for another reason to arrest him.

Morris Hillquit (1869–1933)

Hillquit may not be as well known in contemporary times as other radicals such as Eugene Dennis, John Reed, or Eugene Debs, but he certainly made his mark with the Socialist circle. Besides his affiliation with the Socialist Party, he was also a noted attorney and defended many of those indicted under the Acts. Hillquit was born in Latvia, with Moishe Hillkowitz as his birth name. His family struggled since immigrating to America, and Hillquit went to work at an early age. He joined the Socialist Party, but had hostility against other radical groups and individuals, such as Anarchists, and even other factions of the Socialist Party. His attempts at gaining a political office failed. Hillquit would oppose the U.S. involvement in WWI, and would serve as council to those indicted under the Acts, such as the first trial of *The Masses*. Despite some health problems, he continued to run for mayor of New York City, and to use his position as an attorney to defend fellow radicals. Tuberculosis would get the best of him, and he passed away in 1933.

Judge Julius M. Mayer dismissed another two counts that there was no conspiracy. Nearing was found not guilty, but the ASS was fined $3,000. Like many others, such as Eugene Debs in his trial (to be discussed below), Nearing openly pleaded his case. According to Stephen Whitfield, "Others suspected that Nearing talked his way out of the penitentiary."[8] Regardless, Nearing's case, like that of *The Masses*, was based just as much on celebrity than that of actual violations of federal law.

United States v. Pierce et al. deals with a group of pamphleteers distributing a circular criticizing the draft and the Attorney General. The Circuit Court of Appeals ruled "Any and all resistance and any and all obstruction to the operation and enforcement of a law may be declared an offense."[9] The Circuit Court in United States v. Boutin, ruling on another anti-war and anti-conscription pamphlet, held "May not a jury find that one who promulgates such a doctrine is attempting to cause refusal of duty in the military and naval forces of the United States?"[10] The case of United States v. Baker also examines the difference between general statements and statements which could potentially obstruct the law. District Judge Rose said:

> Every man has a perfect right to any opinion he may see fit to
> form about any proposed law, or about any law that is on the statute
> books . . . So the real injury here is: Can the government show, always
> beyond a reasonable doubt, that these men were trying to persuade
> people to disobey the law?[11]

While there was a national search by many against supposedly dangerous enemies, more than one judge was not so willing to participate in such irrational activities.

No work on the Acts would be complete without the re-telling of the U.S. Supreme Court cases *Schenck v. United States* (1919) and *Abrams v. United States* (1919). While these decisions are certainly part of legal history, parts of these still remain a part of American ideology, with even some phrases being used for fiction and film titles. What contemporary times do not realize is that such catch phrases had a far different meaning than what is currently understood.

The *Schenck* case set a standard that, to this day, has far reaching consequences, including in folklore. The well-known phrase of "clear and present danger" originated from this case, and not from Cold War rhetoric, as most believe. What has been forgotten was how the first amendment rights of free speech were clearly trampled upon.

At the risk of being trite, the events of the case and its decision are very well part of American history. Charles T. Schenck and Elizabeth Baer, both members of the Socialist Party, wrote a pamphlet encouraging disobedience to the draft, believing such a government action to be unfair. One argument they made, and one that had been made before and repeated after, was that the draft was in violation of the Thirteenth amendment, banning slavery or involuntary servitude. Now, and as before, the courts never accepted that argument.

But the Thirteenth amendment argument was not central to the issue. As with the other cases under the Acts, the issue was free speech and the right of a country to successfully conduct a war effort. The conviction was upheld, and in a way that would resound throughout decades.

In 1919 came the infamous Supreme Court decision officially known as *Schenck v. United States*, and *Elizabeth Baer v. United States*, although it is commonly referred to as the *Schenck* case.[12] Outside of the Supreme Court cases of *Marbury v. Madison* and *Sandford v. Scott* have such words resounded throughout U.S. history. The decision against Schenck was a unanimous 9–0. The famous justice Oliver Wendell Holmes delivered the Court's opinion. While recognizing the First Amendment rights to free speech, this right did not apply in this case. By citing "clear and present danger," the actions of the defendants could, in time of war, harm the actions of the government to conduct that war. It was also stated that while one had free speech, it did not give one the right to falsely yell "fire!" in a crowded theater and cause a panic.

However, one distributing pamphlets to a mere estimated 15,000 and yelling in a theater and causing true death can be argued to the end of time. But the Supreme Court battle was not over. The *Abrams* case would solidify, to many, how the ideas of free speech would resound through the years. Whereas most of the major cases involved only the Espionage Act, the *Abrams* case specifically addressed the Sedition Act. The full name of the case is *Jacob Abrams, et al. v. United States*.[13] What makes this case especially interesting is that, while it did involve the war to an extent, it had to do with the Russian Revolution.

The *Abrams* case came about in a manner similar to so many others under the Acts in that two separate leaflets were thrown out of a New York City window by a group of street agitators, one of which was Jacob Abrams. What was so different about these tracts, and what separated them from other writings, were their inflammatory remarks. At the time, 1918, the Bolshevik (Red) control of Russia was not complete. The United States became somewhat involved by sending in troops to support the Anti-Bolshevik forces (White), landing forces in Archangel and Vladivostok. Abrams and his comrades found this appalling.

One of the tracts, in Yiddish, was anti-war, but especially criticized this U.S. involvement in Russia. In addition to admonishing the U.S. for supporting the Whites, thus blocking revolutionary goals, the group demanded that any war material production and use against the Bolsheviks must end. The other leaflet was a slight variation of the first in which it condemned the U.S. landing troops in Russia. Abrams, along with four others, were arrested, indicted, and convicted under the Sedition Act for attempting to curtail production, and, thus, attempting to create resistance to the war effort. The prison sentences ran from 10 to 20 years. The case naturally made its way to the Supreme Court where the decision was interesting in how it was decided.

On November 10, 1919, the Court upheld the convictions by a 7–2 vote, not unanimously as so many other cases under the Acts were decided. The majority opinion was written by Justice John H. Clarke, and that their right to free speech was not violated. Using the "bad tendency" test, Clarke found the pamphlets criticizing the U.S. forces in the Soviet Union as falling within the scope of the Sedition Act. The acts of the defendants were therefore illegal by trying to incite not just actions against the war effort but promote revolutionary fervor within the United States. The "clear and present danger" as stated in the *Schenck* case applied here as well.

The fact that the decision was not unanimous is made even more intriguing by the dissent, which is actually better known than the majority decision written by Clarke. Holmes, joined by Justice Louis Brandeis, wrote the dissent, whereas in the past he wrote the majority opinion in the other cases under the Acts. In his opinion, the defendants were not trying to obstruct the war against Germany, but were merely addressing the situation in Russia. While the defendants certainly made extremely bold statements (including signing one of the pamphlets "Revolutionists"), Holmes did not see his own "clear and present danger" doctrine. Essentially, they were loud, not dangerous, and not even known outside of their own circle of acquaintances.[14]

Other than the *Schenck* and *Abrams* cases, the most famous person indicted, convicted, and imprisoned under the Acts was Eugene V. Debs. Interestingly enough, the conviction during this particular time period was not the first time Debs encountered the Supreme Court. And, in both instances, the Court would not find in his favor.

Debs is remembered most as a Socialist labor leader. Born in 1855 in Terre Haute, Indiana, at an early age he went to work for the railroads. He joined the labor movement and rose quickly through its ranks. In 1893 he helped create the American Railway Union (ARU), becoming its president. He especially made his mark as a radical leader during the infamous Pullman Strike of 1894. An injunction was issued against the ARU, which Debs and other leaders ignored. He was sentenced to 6 months in jail for contempt of court, which was appealed to the Supreme Court. In *In Re Debs*, the Court found against him for violating interstate commerce and transportation of the mails.[15] It is said that when he emerged from jail he was an affirmed

Socialist. However, Nick Salvatore argues that the jailing was just part of a gradual transition to Socialism.[16] His radical career continued when he helped in the founding of the Industrial Workers of the World (IWW) in Chicago in 1905. He ran for president five times on the Socialist ticket, even winning 6 percent of the popular vote in 1912.

But Debs would find himself once more in hot water over WWI. Like many other Socialists, Debs was critical of the war from the onset. Needless to say, Wilson was not pleased with his speeches, and considered Debs to be a traitor. It was on June 16, 1918, Debs made his infamous speech in Canton, Ohio. He stressed that people resist the draft, and praised those who already did so. On June 30, he was arrested under the Espionage Act and charged with 10 counts.

He was convicted on September 12. Debs called no witnesses to his defense. Instead, he was allowed to address the court, whereby he spoke for two hours. Two days later was the sentencing hearing, whereby he once again spoke with a stirring speech. On November 18, he was sentenced to 10 years in prison, as well as losing his voting privileges.

Once again, Debs appealed his case to the Supreme Court. In the 1919 ruling *Debs v. United States*, the Court once again rejected his arguments.[17] Part of the Court's ruling came from similarities to the *Schenck* case. What the Supreme Court could not ignore was that Debs did openly express obstruction to the draft, and had admiration for others who did. On April 13, 1919, Debs went to a federal penitentiary in Atlanta, Georgia.

Amazingly enough, this did not prevent him from running for president in the 1920 election, netting over 200,000 votes. Plus, he was very popular with the other inmates. While clemency was proposed, Wilson did not act on it. The new president, Warren G. Harding, commuted Debs' sentence to time

Eugene V. Debs (1855–1926)

Debs was undoubtedly one of the most highly profiled persons ever convicted under the Acts. While his particular case under the Supreme Court did not have the impact of *Schenck* or *Gitlow*, his national prominence as a radical labor leader certainly gave his situation attention. Starting working for the railroads, he established himself as a national labor leader, although his status later as a Socialist gave him a greater standing as a radical. When Debs ran for president in 1912 on the Socialist ticket, he garnered an incredible 6 percent of the national vote, almost unthinkable for a third (or fourth!) party candidate. His speech in Canton, Ohio, earned him a prison sentence under the Acts. During his time in an Atlanta, Georgia prison he again ran for president, and was popular among his fellow inmates. While Wilson hesitated on his pardon, President Warren G. Harding—himself believing in Debs' guilt—had him released in 1921. Debs still stands as a symbol of working class rights, and how one's prominence could only enhance one's chances of facing problems under the Acts.

served on December 23, 1921. While Harding still thought Debs guilty, the latter's failing health and charm made him likeable. There was a huge roar of support from the other inmates when he exited the prison.[18]

There are other Supreme Court cases arising out of the WWI era and just after that bear mentioning. Many states passed anti-syndicalist laws throughout the years. As mentioned in Chapter 3, Attorney General Thomas Gregory felt he could not use the power of the federal government to prosecute certain activities since no national legislation was in place, and that such cases were better left to the states that had such laws.

While these cases may not be directly related to the Acts, the time period in which they occurred, and the topics involved, fall within the scope of this work. As stated in the beginning of this work, the idea of enforcing patriotism was present since the Era of the New Republic. While it did not pick up the intensity seen until the WWI era, making sure the country was stocked with "good Americans" took on many levels. Three particular cases come to mind: *Meyer v. Nebraska* (1923), *Pierce v. Society of Sisters* (1925), and *Gitlow v. New York* (1925). While the first two addressed foreign culture, the third returned to the idea of revolutionary speech.

The *Meyer* case invoked all too recent memories of hysteria against anything German. Many states passed legislation to spark patriotism, and Nebraska was no exception. On April 9, 1919, that state passed what is known as the Siman Act. Directed at students under the high school level, this particular law banned the teaching of any language other than English in every school, public or private. Previously legislation was considered by the federal Department of Education.

Prior to the passage of the Siman Act, there was concern among many about how the German language was used in Lutheran churches across the nation. Nebraska aimed to curb such use. Robert T. Meyer was arrested on

Thomas Watt Gregory (1861–1933)

If anyone had ambivalent feelings towards the prosecution of foreigners and/or radicals, it was Watt. In his tenure as the United States Attorney General, he would not prosecute any individual if there were no laws giving him that power. Born in Crawfordsville, Mississippi, he, like Wilson, was well educated, practicing law in Texas and even had a tenure as a regent at the University of Texas, he turned down some appointments. In August 1914, Wilson appointed Gregory as Attorney General. As WWI broke out, along with the fear of internal insurrection, Gregory would not proceed with prosecution since there was no federal law giving him that authority. He felt such actions should be performed by the states. But, with the U.S. entry, Gregory helped with the formation of the Acts, even working along with Burleson. Due to his hearing loss, he declined a U.S. Supreme Court appointment. He continued to work along with Wilson. Years after the war ended a bout of pneumonia ended his life.

May 25, 1920 for teaching Raymond Parpart, who was only 10 years old, reading in German. This was one of the old one-room schools, and a Hamilton County official happened by while the instruction was taking place.

Meyers was convicted of violating the Siman Act. His arguments before the Nebraska Supreme failed since they felt the law would protect American society. He would take his case to the U.S. Supreme Court where the June 4, 1923 vote was 7–2 in his favor. Justice James McReynolds wrote the majority opinion, stating that the statute went too far. Although states can determine their own curriculum, they had no power to ban an entire subject. Since there was no war at the time, there was no threat, and that freedoms include the right to speak whatever language one wished. Holmes dissented, believing the law did not violate any Constitutional liberties, and applied only to children. The law did not prevent people using a foreign language in a place other than schools.[19]

The 1925 case of *Pierce v. Society of Sisters* had similar issues to *Meyer*.[20] Like with Nebraska, Oregon wished to preserve the "purity" of American culture, or at least make it as uniform as possible. And, as with Nebraska, Oregon targeted the school system. In a November 7, 1922 act, Oregon voters approved a measure banning all parochial schools. All children between the ages of 8 and 16 were required to attend public school. There were exceptions to having to attend public school, such as those who were state-monitored home schooled, physical limitations to travel, or a private school recognized by the state.

The fact that parochial schools were targeted is not much of a surprise. In terms of U.S. history alone, there was always a strong anti-Catholic bias in the country. While some of it stems from centuries-long feuding between Catholics and Protestants, as the nation began to develop its unique American character, Catholicism was also viewed as anti-American. Even during the American Revolution there were thoughts that if Catholic France were to assist in the struggle they would then try to convert the country. While most of the Protestant denominations had their own "headquarters" in the States, the Catholic Church was seated in a foreign country run by a foreign leader. This was further exacerbated by the re-emergence of the Ku Klux Klan (KKK) in 1916, who especially targeted Catholics.

Along with Hill Military Academy, who felt the economic sting of dropping enrollment rates, the Sisters of the Holy Names sued, including naming Oregon governor Walter Pierce in the suit, and obtaining an injunction against the case. The two plaintiffs won their case, and the state appealed to the Supreme Court in 1925. With a June 1 decision of that same year, Oregon would find itself on the losing end of a unanimous decision.

Once again writing for the Supreme Court, McReynolds held the law was an unreasonable interference of the right of parents to educate their children. The issue of compulsory education was not even at stake (that being a major goal of the Progressive Era). The state could not determine what types of school a child should attend, only that they must go. This decision would set a precedent for decades to come.

Gitlow v. New York, also in 1925, returned to the idea of whether the government could suppress radical publications based upon certain criteria. Decided at the height of the First Red Scare (See Chapter 5), the *Gitlow* case had roots extended back decades. Many states across the country passed "criminal anarchy statutes," which greatly suppressed any radical publications, whether or not revolutionary, beginning in the late nineteenth century, long before WWI. Especially spurred on by the Haymarket Riot of 1886 (See Chapter 1), the fear of radicalism, especially Marxist-based, was very real. What did differ between the states was their definition of "criminal anarchy," what constituted a revolutionary tract, and how to punish those who disseminated such writings.

New York had such a law since 1902. Benjamin Gitlow was a member of the Socialist Party, and had once served in the New York State Assembly, went to trial in January 1920, for a piece entitled *Left Wing Manifesto*, published the previous year. He was convicted on February 11, 1920, with a prison sentence of 5 to 10 years. Upon appeal he was out on bail after 2 years, and his case wound up before the Supreme Court. He was defended by the fairly recent organization American Civil Liberties Union (ACLU). Gitlow would lose his case by a 7–2 vote.

The opinion by Justice Edward T. Sanford addressed the issue of a state law could prohibit certain kinds of publications that advocated the overthrow of the government. Although Gitlow's defense held the piece did not do so, the Court disagreed, and held such a law was valid, and that Gitlow violated that law. As with the *Abrams* case, the "bad tendency" test was applied, and the state had a right to protect itself. And, as with *Abrams*, Holmes dissented. As part of his dissent, Holmes pointed out that Gitlow was hardly a threat to mainstream society as few, if any, knew of him outside his immediate circle.[21]

In so many ways, the Acts of WWI were not an original idea when it came to suppressing supposed radical ideologies, stretching back into the nineteenth century. Nor were these about to end with the end of the war. As the cases involving the WWI fears continued, so did the fear that while the war was over, the threat from internal disruption was not.

It is easy to go throughout legal and legislative history and see how the law grows and develops over time. There are examples that fill whole volumes. This work is merely an overview to provide the reader with an idea of what happened during the WWI era.

Benjamin Gitlow (1891–1965)

Gitlow's name is on the title of one of the most important U.S. Supreme Court cases in history. Indicted and convicted under the Acts, Gitlow's case upheld and enhanced the "clear and present danger" doctrine established under the *Schenck v. United States* case. Born in New Jersey, Gitlow was introduced to radical doctrine at an early age. He later joined the Socialist Party, even winning a seat in the New York legislature. Due to his connection with *The Revolutionary Age*, a radical newspaper, and his belief in revolution, he was convicted and imprisoned under the Acts. Although sentenced for 5 to 10 years in prison, and spending 3 years free on bail, he did not serve the full term and was pardoned. Despite having helped form the Communist Party of the United States, Gitlow was eventually disillusioned with radicalism and became a staunch conservative, even testifying before the House Committee on Un-American Activities (HUAC) against Communism. He would die in New York.

But it wasn't over yet. While the Sedition Act was set to expire, the Espionage Act continued, although watered down by changes and court decisions. There was more to take place, and some believed the worst was yet to come.

NOTES

1 Woodrow Wilson, letter to Albert Sydney Burleson, Postmaster General, October 11, 1917, Albert S. Burleson Papers, Vol. 19, Manuscript Collection, Library of Congress, Washington, D.C.
2 Max Eastman, *Love and Revolution* (New York: Random House, 1964), 85.
3 "A Talk With Mr. Burleson," *New York Evening Post*, November 21, 1917, Albert S. Burleson Papers, Container 18.
4 Albert S. Burleson, Letter to the Editor of the *Washington Post*, 1 November 1919, Albert S. Burleson Papers, Vol. 25.
5 John A. Saltmarsh, *Scott Nearing: The Making of a Homesteader* (White River Junction, VT: Chelsea Green Publishing, 1998), 158.
6 Ibid.
7 *United States v. Nearing*, 252 Federal Reporter, 230, District Court, N.D., New York, August 1, 1918. See also Stephen J. Whitfield, *Scott Nearing: Apostle of American Radicalism* (New York: Columbia University Press, 1974).
8 John A. Saltmarsh, Scott Nearing: The Making of a Homesteader (White River Junction, VT: Chelsea Green Publishing, 1998), 117.
9 *United States v. Pierce et al.*, 245 Federal Reporter, 888, District Court, N.D., New York, November 7, 1917.
10 *United States v. Boutin*, 251 Federal Reporter, 316, District Court, N.D., May 11, 1918.
11 *United States v. Baker et al.*, 247 Federal Reporter, 124, District Court, N.D., Maryland, July 11, 1917.
12 *Charles T. Schenck v. United States, Elizabeth Baer v. United States*, 249 U.S. 47.
13 *Jacob Abrams, et al. v. United States*, 250 U.S. 616, 1919.

14   For an excellent source concerning Holmes, see Thomas Healy, *The Great Dissent: How Oliver Wendell Holmes Changed His Mind—And Changed the History of Free Speech in America* (New York: Henry Holt, 2013).

15   *In Re Debs*, 158 U.S. 564.

16   Nick Salvatore, *Eugene V. Debs: Citizen and Socialist* (Urbana, IL: University of Illinois Press, 2007).

17   *Debs v. United States*. 249 U.S. 211.

18   See Richard Polenberg, *Fighting Faiths: The Abrams Case, the Supreme Court, and Free Speech* (Ithaca, NY: Cornell University Press, 1999); and Stephen A. Smith, "Schenck v. United States and Abrams v. United States," in Richard A. Parker, Ed., *Free Speech on Trial: Communication Perspectives on Landmark Supreme Court Decisions* (Tuscaloosa, AL: University of Alabama Press, 2003), 20–35.

19   *Meyer v. Nebraska*, 262 U.S. 390, 1923. See also Christopher Capozzola, *Uncle Sam Wants You: World War I and the Making of the Modern American Citizen* (Oxford, UK: Oxford University Press, 2008).

20   The full case name *is Pierce, Governor of Oregon, et al. v. Society of the Sisters of the Holy Names of Jesus and Mary*, 268 U.S. 510, 1925.

21   *Benjamin Gitlow v. People of the State of New York*, 268 U.S. 652, 1925. See also Geoffrey R. Stone, *Perilous Times: Free Speech in Wartime from the Sedition Act of 1798 to the War on Terrorism* (New York: W.W. Norton, 2004); Mark Lendler, *Gitlow v. New York: Every Idea an Incitement* (Lawrence, KS: University Press of Kansas, 2012).

BIBLIOGRAPHY

Albert S. Burleson, Letter to the Editor of the *Washington Post*, November 1, 1919, Albert S. Burleson Papers, Vol. 25.

"A Talk With Mr. Burleson," *New York Evening Post*, November 21, 1917, Albert S. Burleson Papers, Container 18.

Benjamin Gitlow v. People of the State of New York, 268 U.S. 652, 1925.

Capozzola, Christopher. *Uncle Sam Wants You: World War I and the Making of the Modern American Citizen*. Oxford, UK: Oxford University Press, 2008.

Charles T. Schenck v. United States, Elizabeth Baer v. United States. 249 U.S. 47.

Debs v. United States. 249 U.S. 211.

Eastman, Max. *Love and Revolution*. New York: Random House, 1964.

Healy, Thomas. *The Great Dissent: How Oliver Wendell Holmes Changed His Mind—And Changed the History of Free Speech in America*. New York: Henry Holt, 2013.

In Re Debs. 158 U.S. 564.

Jacob Abrams, et al. v. United States, 250 U.S. 616, 1919.

Lendler, Mark. *Gitlow v. New York: Every Idea an Incitement*. Lawrence, KS: University Press of Kansas.

Meyer v. Nebraska, 262 U.S. 390, 1923.

Polenberg, Richard. *Fighting Faiths: The Abrams Case, the Supreme Court, and Free Speech*. Ithaca, NY: Cornell University Press, 1999.

Saltmarsh, John A. *Scott Nearing: The Making of a Homesteader*. White River Junction, VT: Chelsea Green Publishing, 1998.

Salvatore, Nick. *Eugene V. Debs: Citizen and Socialist*. Urbana, IL: University of Illinois Press, 2007.

Smith, Stephen A. "Schenck v. United States and Abrams v. United States," in Richard A. Parker, Ed., *Free Speech on Trial: Communication Perspectives on Landmark Supreme Court Decisions*, 20–35. Tuscaloosa, AL: University of Alabama Press, 2003.

Stone, Geoffrey R. *Perilous Times: Free Speech in Wartime from the Sedition Act of 1798 to the War on Terrorism*. New York: W.W. Norton, 2004.

United States v. Baker et al. 247 Federal Reporter, 124.

United States v. Boutin. 251 Federal Reporter, 316.

United States v. Nearing. 252 Federal Reporter, 230.

United States v. Pierce et al. 245 Federal Reporter, 888.

Whitfield, Stephen J. *Scott Nearing: Apostle of American Radicalism*. New York: Columbia University Press, 1974.

Woodrow Wilson, letter to Albert Sydney Burleson, Postmaster General, October 11, 1917, Albert S. Burleson Papers, Vol. 19, Manuscript Collection, Library of Congress, Washington, D.C.

CHAPTER 5

Aftermath

As opposed to World War II (WWII), WWI had no defining final events. WWII had the 1944 invasion of Normandy to spark the beginning of the end for Germany, especially ending with Adolph Hitler's suicide, as well as the 1945 atomic bombs being used on Japan. WWI more or less petered out, with Germany making a peace move in 1918.

It has been said more than once that winning the peace was/is as essential as winning the war itself. When the peace negotiations began in Paris in 1919, countries from literally around the world felt they could share in the spoils of war, even if they did not participate in the actual conflict. Colonized countries—such as those in Asia and Africa—believed that this "war for democracy" and later "self-determination" would apply to them. These hopes would soon be dashed. These colonial areas would remain under control until after WWII.

The Sedition Act applied only to wartime. On December 13, 1920, this act was in fact repealed. However, the Espionage Act was still in force, as was the fear of dissent, both foreign and domestic.

Someone had to take the blame for the war, and Germany was the foil, even though that country was not responsible for the start of hostilities, yet was made to pay in so many ways for its horrific results. Then came the idea of maintaining the peace. This was also easier said than done. Wilson's idea for a League of Nations would be created, but, of course, ultimately fail, with even the United States refusing to join. While the war was officially over, the underlying problems still persisted. There were still "upstart" nations that could cause more world problems. But for the U.S., another problem remained. While winning the peace was as imperative as winning WWI, there was the continuing war at home against internal dissent.

1919 might well be considered the year that the country truly felt threatened from both within and through outside forces. The two Russian revolutions of 1917 were merely the start. While the first revolution ousted Tsar Nicholas II, it was the Bolshevik revolution later that year that especially had far reaching effects. First, the Bolsheviks took Russia out of WWI, and the fact they were a Marxist-ideology posed a threat to Western capitalist society.

As related in Chapter 3, the potential that radicals could have a negative influence on the conduct of the war made so many people suspect. With the Communist takeover of Russia, turning it into the Soviet Union, there were fears of a similar uprising in the U.S. and 1919 was just the year when many believed radicals might succeed in overthrowing the government and the American way of life.[1] The retributions were swift and powerful. For the purposes of this discussion, we will proceed thematically.

The Palmer Raids of 1920 is what is most identified as the start of the first Red Scare. With the Bolshevik revolution still very fresh in the minds of the Western capitalist world, there were fears that a similar action was about to occur in the country. Leftist revolutions in Europe first gave a scare in 1848, the same year *The Communist Manifesto* was published. However, as noted in Chapter 1, Marxist-based radicalism was not perceived as a true threat in the U.S. until well after the Civil War. With the onset of the twentieth century, and the Russian revolutions, the federal government began its clampdown on radical groups. The Palmer Raids was just that start.

Ever since the Bolsheviks took control of Russia, and renamed it the Soviet Union, they began a propaganda campaign to Marxist radicals around the world, especially targeting the Western nations. With trials under the Acts still underway, and convicted people behind prison bars, the Palmer Raids served as a reminder to any dissenters they were not out of the woods—they were still under scrutiny.

Orchestrated by Attorney General A. Mitchell Palmer (see overleaf for short biography) and the United States Department of Justice, thousands of radicals—real or perceived—were subjected to arrest, detainment, and, for some, deportation. The Palmer Raids have been depicted in some Hollywood films, such as *Reds* (1981) and *J. Edgar* (2011). In the former, sympathies lie with the radicals, while in the latter, motives for the operations were explained and justified, at least in the eyes of a true patriotic American. However one felt about Palmer's actions, he was not without his critics in the federal government itself.

Palmer appeared before the House Appropriations Committee in June 1919, requesting a larger budget in order to combat those who would destroy the American government. His request for a $2 million budget from his current $1.5 million budget was denied, although he was granted a $100,000 increase. While this small increase may have seemed like a disappointment, Palmer nevertheless began to make his moves against the

Alexander (A.) Mitchell Palmer (1872–1936)

Generally referred to as A. Mitchell Palmer, he is best remembered as Attorney General of the United States from 1919 to 1921, and for his repeated attacks on the radical sector. Following Thomas Watt Gregory in that office, also appointed by President Wilson, he had a long career in politics as a member of the Democratic Party. With the sinking of the *Lusitania* in 1915, he hoped that incident would not be a reason for war. However, once the United States entered WWI, he served on a local draft board, eventually working for Wilson as the Alien Property Custodian, a post that dealt with the property of enemies in the country during the war. Palmer was then appointed as Attorney General. While he was instrumental in releasing over 10,000 people of German descent who had been detained, he turned to the suppression of radicalism. An assassination attempt through the use of a mail bomb failed. In the Department of Justice, he began the General Intelligence Unit, utilizing the skills of J. Edgar Hoover, who would go on to his own prominence. Believing the radical sector posed a threat to the safety of the country, a series of raids under Palmer began in 1919 (known as the "Palmer Raids"). Thousands were arrested, and while a large number were set free, hundreds of immigrants were deported. When calmer times prevailed, he attempted to run for future office, but with failure.

radical community, not realizing this was hardly a solid movement but one filled with as many divisions as in mainstream political culture.

The following month Palmer conducted the first of his many raids. Occurring in Buffalo, New York, a group of anarchists were arrested. A federal judge dismissed the charges, especially since they came from a nineteenth-century law. The Acts were not even an issue here. The judge saw no violent threat from these particular anarchists since they advocated evolution and not revolution, with words as their most potent weapon.

Palmer was not deterred. He realized he needed to approach his actions from a more stringent legal standpoint, and to utilize other government agencies and officials. Within his own organization Palmer made a move. On August 1, 1919, this action would resonate throughout American history for decades. A young J. Edgar Hoover was appointed to head up the Bureau of Investigation, with the main charge of monitoring radical groups. Eventually becoming the Federal Bureau of Investigation (FBI), Hoover will always be remembered for his actions to bring elements of the criminal community to justice. For the moment, the radicals would be his main focus.

To be expected, Hoover's first order of business was to collect information on as many radicals as possible. As stated by Howard N. Meyer, "Agents were instructed to collect what they could from private individuals and companies, from local and state police and other authorities."[2] With this information in hand, "the stage was set for the Big Red Raid." Palmer and Hoover were preparing for the push to try to eliminate radicals in the country once and for all.[3]

Palmer would also turn to the Department of Labor. Since the Buffalo anarchists were let off the hook, and Palmer knew, as stated, he needed to use other legal means to combat radicalism, he hoped the Secretary of Labor would provide assistance, since it was through that office that warrants could be issued against those violating immigration laws, as well as signing deportation papers. But the Senate was not thoroughly convinced of Palmer's plans, and passed a unanimous resolution on October 17 demanding an explanation of his actions. That explanation was not immediately forthcoming, and Palmer was just about to start his program in earnest.

It was the autumn of 1919 that Palmer made his first serious moves against the radicals. The second anniversary of the Bolshevik Revolution was coming up on November 7, and this would be a prime opportunity to strike at perceived enemies of the state. Working along with local law enforcement agencies, the Bureau of Investigation launched raids against the Union of Russian Workers in no less than 12 cities. The raids did not stop with this Union but continued against American citizens as well, especially those who were of Russian descent, and who just happened to be in the area at the time. Other political and labor agitators were seized as well, and it is reported that the number of warrants issued were less than those actually arrested. More importantly, reports of violence, especially severe beatings, came out. Many claimed they were beaten in order to force a confession. This was all well publicized in the media.

Palmer eventually presented his actions to the Senate. In an apparent precursor to Senate Joe McCarthy's statements during the Second Red Scare of the 1950s, Palmer also claimed to have had over 60,000 names of people who were considered dangerous to the well-being of the country. He also pointed out he was following the letter of the law by acting through the Department of Labor, although that agency was not convinced of the necessity of the raids. Secretary of Labor William B. Wilson did not believe that merely belonging to an organization constituted a crime. To Hoover this was not a deterrent and he used other Department of Labor workers to obtain the warrants desired.

In a sad turn of events, using the established federal law, arrested aliens were subjected to deportation. On December 22, 1919, the USS Buford sailed with 249 deportees aboard. The two most famous of those deported were Emma Goldman (also depicted in the film Reds) and Alexander Berkman, both avowed Anarchists, and both spent 2 years in prison for violating the Espionage Act.[4] Called the Soviet Ark, the Buford carried away, with great fanfare from many throughout the country, a foreign presence that many felt should not have been allowed into the country in the first place.[5]

Beginning on January 2, 1920, under the direction of Hoover, the next series of mass raids took place, lasting several days at first, but eventually

Emma Goldman (1869–1940)

Arguably the most famous female Anarchist of all time, Goldman exemplified the very ideal of a fiery feminist who never feared to defy any sort of social norms. Having immigrated to the United States in 1885, she was attracted to Anarchism after the Chicago Haymarket Riot of 1886. She would for several years find herself behind bars many times, especially for trying to "incite to riot." Goldman was partly implicated in the assassination of President William McKinley in 1901. There was no evidence to suggest thus, and she was released. Goldman promoted a very radical agenda that went against current Victorian Era norms, especially concerning birth control. A prolific writer and speaker, Goldman already had a "notorious" reputation when WWI broke out, it almost appeared that the authorities were waiting for the single opportunity to arrest her. Her anti-war activities got her arrested in the summer of 1917, and, under the Espionage Act, she was sentenced to 2 years in prison. When the first Red Scare hit upon the post-WWI years, Goldman, despite being a naturalized U.S. citizen, was deported in December of 1919 on the infamous "Soviet Ark." She died in 1940, and was since immortalized in the 1981 Warren Beatty film *Reds*, whereby actress Maureen Stapleton won Best Supporting Actress for her role as Goldman.

lasting over 6 weeks. By now the Communists were especially targeted, even though they, like the IWW, were not a united group at this time. The raids were carried out in over 33 cities in 23 states, and the estimates on the number of those arrested range from 2,700 to over 3,000. Many of those arrested were held for extended periods of time.

Palmer was not without his supporters. As with the Merritt Conspiracy law in Illinois discussed in Chapter 1, many still argued that agitators must be held accountable for their actions, especially such actions that led to violence and posed a threat to the established way of life. Others continued to cry for more stringent immigration laws, because, to them, it was obvious foreigners were nothing but agitators and should be kept out of the country. As for natural born agitators, especially the troublemakers in the labor movement, even while they were born in the country, their very actions moved to disrupt the American way of life. If they wanted to rally against millionaires, they could work hard and become one as well, instead of trying to take away an employer's hard-earned property.

Many believed by May that the raids were officially over, but in April 1920, a small political battle was brewing. Louis Freeland Post began to serve as Acting Secretary of Labor, and he made it clear he was not going to be the puppet of Palmer and Hoover. While deportations continued, Post canceled over 2,000 warrants since he believed them to be illegal. Attempts to remove Post from office were unsuccessful, including an appeal to President Wilson. Palmer's continued attacks on radicals began to seem as nothing but paranoia as projected uprisings never materialized. Furthermore, the legal community rallied against Palmer's actions, and many courts set free detained prisoners.[6] Like McCarthy in the 1950s, many saw Palmer as a joke, and Palmer's attempt in 1920 to obtain the Democratic Party's nomination for president was an utter failure.

At the start of WWI, there was no Communist party per se in the country, for the Socialist Party (SPA) tended to represent the Marxist-based thinkers (this is not taking into consideration people like Anarchists and various splinter groups), while the dilemma faced by the Socialist Party over any sort of support or rejection of WWI presented numerous problems, none more so than that of support for the Russian Bolsheviks. This would set in motion an issue that would be part of American society for decades.

The left wing section of the SPA (if there can be such a thing) supported the Bolsheviks.

> Differences of opinion are only natural, especially with Lenin's January 1919 invitation for the left wing of the SPA to participate in the founding of the Communist Third International, also known as the Comintern. However, the SPA had expelled certain sections of the party, and those who were expelled and supported the Bolsheviks met in June 1919 to return to the party.[7]

Led by Louis Fraina and Charles Ruthenberg, a segment broke away and formed the Communist Party of America on September 2, 1919.

John Reed and Benjamin Gitlow moved to take over the SPA convention. It would not be successful, especially with the police ready to move in on them. On September 1, just one day before Fraina's actions, the Communist Labor Party was created in Chicago, the same place as Fraina's group. These two competing Communist groups sought recognition from Moscow, who refused to do so until they combined, which they did so in 1921. This was re-enacted in Warren Beatty's Academy Award winning film *Reds* (1981). However, both Communist parties were immediately forced to go underground.

What also scared mainstream America was the massive strike wave across the country in 1919. It is estimated that one-fifth of all workers went on strike, approximately 4 million. During WWI, in order to keep the war machine running, many workers were on a "no strike" pledge. With the war's conclusion, and the increasing loss of benefits, worker frustration grew. Seattle became the center of discontent in January 1919, when over 65,000 workers went on strike, and eventually overtook the city. This was not a violent move and the workers actually conducted city business on a peaceful basis. The strike eventually ended, but the Seattle workers had made a bold statement.

Similar strikes broke out in other areas. The steel strike, which took place in 10 cities and involved over 350,000 workers, still remains the subject of many works. In Boston, police officers went on strike in retaliation for the suspension of fellow officers for trying to affiliate with the American Federation of Labor (AFL). Calvin Coolidge, current Massachusetts governor and future president, fired the entire police force, using state troops to maintain order.

While the Communists were forced underground immediately, the one group who was an easy target for the government was the IWW. In his 1928 novel *Boston*, Upton Sinclair writes of a pre-WWI cordage plant strike. Many labor and radical groups were present. These included the AFL, SPA, and

> the Industrial Workers of the World with their speakers, and their program of "direct action," the taking over of the industries by the "one big union." They were strong . . . having the prestige of a great victory in the woolen mills of Lawrence three or four years ago.[8]

Though by 1928, The Industrial Workers of the World (IWW) had long since deteriorated as an effective group, this statement by one of America's premier Socialist writers serves as a focal point.

Organized in 1905, the IWW, whose members were referred to as "Wobblies," immediately presented itself as a group on the outer fringes of labor organization.[9] Distrustful of labor associations such as the AFL, the IWW made itself known to the world as the true workingman's brotherhood. Borrowing heavily from Marxist, anarchist, and socialist ideologies, the IWW reached out to all segments of the working society. Whereas groups such as the AFL were seen as tools of the capitalists, designed to keep the workers docile, the IWW told the unorganized laborer that he would be his own captain. He would work for his own benefit and enjoy the fruits of his labor.

The road was long and difficult. To the IWW, the exclusion of unskilled labor, a habit practiced by the AFL, was not only a sham but a crime. Craft unionism served only to alienate and divide workers. By organizing along industrial lines, that is, according to each industry as a whole rather than according to individual positions within each industry, workers would act under a banner of solidarity, striving for the benefit of all. According to their preamble of 1905, "The trade workers foster a state of affairs which allows one set of workers to be pitted against another set of workers in the same industry, thereby helping defeat one another in wage wars."[10] But as the IWW discovered, as so many labor groups before, organizing the lower working classes took more skill, power, and finance than originally believed. Despite their overall failure as a labor, and radical, organization, the IWW was looked upon with scorn and fear.

Assessing the membership strength of the IWW is difficult. According to Patrick Renshaw,

> membership rarely exceeded 100,000 at any one time. On the other hand, the turnover in members was so high, averaging 133 percent a year from 1905–1915, that as many as one million workers held IWW cards, and were exposed to IWW propaganda, at one time in their lives.[11]

That these numbers, when taken in contrast to the whole of the working-class population in the early twentieth century, is alarmingly low, one must wonder why the IWW was a feared institution.

The IWW hobbled through internal dissent, violent attacks, strike failures, and the inability to reach out to the working class as a whole. A longtime subject of government scrutiny, the IWW suffered persecution by the Department of Justice under the Acts. Facing over 2,000 criminal charges, over 100 of its members were tried and convicted. They were fined, imprisoned, or both.[12]

There were other reasons to wonder why the IWW was considered dangerous. A major problem was the split between those believing in anarchist techniques and those who relied on more peaceful measures to achieve their goals. This issue forced out numerous leaders, such as famed Socialist Daniel DeLeon, and more rank-and-file members, such as Ralph Chapin (to be discussed below). Another problem was geographical. The Wobblies of the West were far more insurrectionist than those of the East. Eventually this debate ruptured the movement as a whole.

It could easily be argued that the persecution of the IWW began immediately upon its inception. Its far left ideologies, however much they presented a disagreement among its members, still posed a threat to the AFL, which was still struggling for mainstream acceptance. However, the AFL did not want to be seen as anti-American, whereas the IWW promoted a worldwide labor movement agenda, and one that involved foreign ideologies.

The free speech fights involving the IWW's organizing activities are already well documented. But perhaps the first true persecution against the IWW came with the trial of IWW troubadour Joe Hill, whose songs were popular with the movement. Accused of murder under flimsy and unsubstantiated evidence in 1914, and convicted under the same, Hill was executed by a firing squad in 1915. Although his death provided his reputation with a sense of martyrdom, his execution in Utah also served as a reminder to the radical community from government entities they would not be treated with kid gloves. This was further accentuated in 1917 when IWW member

Frank Little was lynched in Butte, Montana, for his anti-war views. As noted, many of the Palmer Raids were directed against the IWW. But the IWW was subjected to raids even earlier, for in 1917 the Department of Justice raided dozens of IWW offices, seizing materials, and resulting in numerous convictions under the Espionage Act (see Chapter 4). With the Palmer Raids now over, and calmer times somewhat returned, the IWW still seemed decimated when one considers the number of years directed against its existence.

However, contemporaries of the first Red Scare were not without those who supported the actions of the government, especially when it came to the IWW. In 1920, Joseph Mereto published *The Red Conspiracy* in order to appeal to the sensibilities of the nation regarding the "Red Peril." Mereto hopes his work will "enable [the workingman] easily to understand the fallacies of the Revolutionists and at the same time make them realize the serious dangers that would result from the adoption of any of the various radical programs."[13]

Mereto sympathizes with the workingman, especially under adverse conditions, but he vehemently distrusts any organization that threatens the current capitalist system. In describing the IWW, he writes

> The IWW, or the so-called "Industrial Workers of the World," whose policy may be summed up in the words, "I Want to Wreck," and who in derision are termed the "I Won't Work," the "Imported Weary Willies," and the "Wobblies," enjoy the unenviable reputation of being classed among the most insurrectionary, imperious and infamous workers of the world to-day.[14]

Mereto sees the IWW as purely anarchist, and states "the Industrial Workers of the World is a revolutionary organization in the strictest sense and has for its object the overthrow of the United States government."[15] To prove his point he presents a "list" of IWW sabotage tactics, ranging from placing acid in machinery to open warfare.

In contrast to Mereto, there is Paul Brissenden's *The IWW: A Study of American Syndicalism*, published first in 1919 and revised in 1920 (later reprinted in 1957). Brissenden, a social scientist, wrote this work during the IWW trials, believing that "for thirteen years the IWW has been rather consistently misrepresented. The public has not been told the truth about the things the IWW has done or the doctrines in which it believes."[16] To Brissenden, the IWW is not an organization to be feared. Rather, it is "what it always has been, a small union."[17] Though he certainly believes the IWW "asks too much when they ask that the producers be given exclusive control of industry," he tries to assure his readers that "they are grossly unprepared for responsibility."[18] More importantly, their talk of sabotage is merely to "whisper it as a footnote, as it were, to their strident blackface statement about method."[19]

But many might not have truly understood how the IWW stood on the war. Certainly, as mentioned, the left wing radical sector not only denounced the war but saw it as a vindication of Marxist doctrine. As Michael Kazin points out, the IWW

> took no official stand against going to war or cooperating with the draft that soon followed. But neither did the Wobblies refrain from calling on workers to keep up the class struggle, regardless of what impact their actions might have on the war effort.[20]

But what about those who were actually part of the First Red Scare? Chapter 4 highlighted actual court cases that arose under the Acts. In 1948, former Wobbly Ralph Chaplin published his record of radical life entitled *Wobbly: The Rough-and-Tumble Story of an American Radical*. An engaging autobiography, Chaplin recounts his years as a revolutionary starting with influences well into his childhood. The son of a struggling worker and often-time farmer, Chaplin's radical influences were fueled early on by a voracious appetite for reading. As a child, Chaplin loved history, and was recounted with tales of frontier battles. Born in 1887, he saw his father take place in the Pullman Strike, and witnessed the pitched battles between frustrated workers and merciless thugs hired by greedy bosses. It was also his first glimpse of Eugene Debs.

Chaplin first encountered socialism through a tract pushed under the door of his family's apartment. Not long after he saw his first Socialist speaker on a soapbox, he became a soapbox speaker himself. Chaplin recalls that

> My father viewed my soapboxing with disapproval. "Socialists," he told me one day, "won't get you anywhere in this country. There might be a future for you in politics but not with the Socialists. You don't have a foreign accent. Why don't you try the Republican party? Maybe they could find a place for you."[21]

While attempting to establish a career as an artist, Chaplin continued his pursuit of radical activities, eventually becoming exposed to syndicalist thought. He soon became an active member of the IWW, not only organizing for the group but also contributing as a songwriter. He was one of the Wobblies indicted during the WWI Espionage Trials, serving a brief prison term until his presidential pardon was granted.

It was easier to brand the IWW than to investigate. Though the use of sabotage was not advocated by all, the distinction was inconsequential to the United States government. To most of the IWW, the use of sabotage involved the stopping of machinery or production, rather than the use of dynamite, as advocated by the most extreme members. In short, their aim was to stop the capitalist system at the point of production. But this contrast was not made during the IWW trial. "The prosecution used the historic meaning of the word to prove we drove spikes into logs, copper tacks into fruit trees, and practiced all manner of arson, dynamiting, and wanton destruction."[22] Factional disputes within the IWW were not the issue; semantics were more important. Like many others, Chaplin later recanted many of his radical beliefs.

One person who held on to his Socialist beliefs was Debs. Although Wilson once considered Debs to be a traitor, he held a certain admirable status among many in the country. While serving his 10-year sentence in an Atlanta, Georgia penitentiary, Debs ran for president, once again, on the Socialist ticket in 1920. The field was quite full that year. Warren G. Harding, nominated by the Republican Party, was seen as the perfect repudiation of those tired of Wilsonian politics. James M. Cox and future president Franklin D. Roosevelt headed the Democratic ticket. Other political parties put forth nominees, such as the Single Tax and the Prohibition parties.

But in the midst of the Palmer Raids and First Red Scare, two parties with radical agendas still went forward: The Socialist Party, and the Farmer-Labor Party (FLP), the latter of which was created by the Chicago Federation of Labor (CFL). The SP and the CFL had a long-standing feud when the CFL first began entering into politics on a serious basis, with the latter beating the former in local Chicago elections in 1919.[23]

The Socialists believed they had the lock on the labor vote and resented an intrusion by an organization they believed should stick merely to labor organizing and leave the political work to others. Despite the CFL's first victories over the Socialists, it was the latter who had the last laugh. With the presidential election of 1920, Harding easily won, with Cox in second, and Debs, from his prison cell, came in third. Parker Parley Christensen, the FLP candidate, received just over 26,000 votes compared to Debs' count of nearly 1 million.

It is interesting to note that while the First Red Scare was occurring with severe crackdowns, the public gave neither of these radical political parties a thought. It raises the question how much this "scare" really scared the public? Daniel Donalson points out how private groups went after radicals, but the American people went after radicals by ignoring them at the polls.[24]

President Wilson considered releasing Debs from prison, even asking Palmer his opinion. It is a matter of debate as to whether Palmer believed in releasing prisoners under the Acts. Debs was elderly by this time, and despite Palmer's suggestion of a presidential pardon, which Wilson denied, it wasn't until Harding became president that Debs was released, his sentence only commuted on December 23, 1921. No pardon was granted. What is well known is that when Debs was released his fellow inmates broke out into a round of cheers. Debs passed away a few years later on October 20, 1926.[25]

Probably one of the most important issues surrounding the aftermath of WWI was the ever-present subject of immigration reform. Since alien residents—legal or not—were blamed for much of the internal anti-war dissent, so must new laws be put in place to make sure any new trouble-makers and undesirables be kept out of the country. While immigration reform laws extend well back into American history, a new chapter was about to begin.

The Emergency Quota Act of 1921 limited the number of immigrants in proportion to the 1910 census. In 1924 came the National Origins Act, also known as the Johnson-Reed Act, which took an even stronger stance against immigrants from places such as Eastern Europe and Asia. While the law was not without its opposition, it remained in force until 1952. For the moment, it seemed that while the problem concerning troublemaking immigrants had not completely gone, at least it was being kept in check.[26]

The radicals were being kept under control, at least for the time being. The so-called "Roaring Twenties" were in full swing. Easy money was seemed to be made, sexual mores were disappearing as people were openly exploring in ways never before seen, movies and radio captivated audiences, as did going to clubs and dancing with members of the opposite sex without any chaperones.

Who cared about radicals? All they did was make noise, and the country learned to ignored them—at least for the time being. It was only a matter of time before the country once again feared radicalism enough to take drastic measures to put such people in their place, preferably prison.

NOTES

1   See Mitchell Newton-Matza, "Reformers, Radicals and Socialists," in *Jazz Age: People and Perspectives* (Santa Barbara, CA: ABC-CLIO, 2009).
2   Howard N. Meyer, *The Amendment that Refused to Die* (Boston, MA: Beacon Press, 1978), 183.
3   Ibid., 184.
4   Goldman and Berkman founded the No Conscription League. They were arrested on June 15, 1917 for conspiring to encourage people not to register for the draft. Goldman personally addressed the jury, but to no avail. Part of their punishment was the possibility of being deported upon release from prison.

5   For a short essay on these raids, see Joyce L. Kornbluth, *Rebel Voices: An IWW Anthology* (Chicago, IL: Charles H. Kerr, 1988), 324.

6   See Zecharia Chafee, *Freedom of Speech* (New York: Harcourt, Brace & Company, 1948) for a great contemporary account of this first Red Scare.

7   Ibid., 143.

8   Upton Sinclair, *Boston* (New York: Albert & Charles Boni, 1928), 65.

9   There are many theories as to how the term *Wobbly* came about, none of which were proven.

10   IWW Preamble, www.iww.org/culture/official/preamble.shtml.

11   Patrick Renshaw, *The Wobblies: The Story of Syndicalism in the United States* (New York: Doubleday & Company, 1967), 22.

12   See Henry E. McGuckin, *Memoirs of a Wobbly* (Chicago, IL: Charles H. Kerr, 1987), for an interesting first-person look at what it meant to be a Wobbly.

13   Joseph Mereto, *The Red Conspiracy* (New York: The National Historical Society, 1920), iii.

14   Ibid., 105.

15   Ibid., 137.

16   Paul Brissenden, *The IWW: A Study of American Syndicalism* (New York: Russell & Russell, 1919), xv.

17   Ibid., vii.

18   Ibid., xx.

19   Ibid., xxi.

20   Michael Kazin, *American Dreamers: How the Left Changed America* (New York: Alfred A. Knopf, 2011), 147.

21   Ralph Chaplin, *Wobbly: The Rough-and-Tumble Story of an American Radical* (Chicago, IL: University of Chicago Press, 1948), 52.

22   Ibid., 207.

23   See Mitchell Newton-Matza, *Intelligent and Honest Radicals: The Chicago Federation and the Politics of Progression* (Lanham, MD: Lexington Books, 2013), Chapter 3.

24   See Daniel Donalson, *The Espionage and Sedition Acts of World War I: Using Wartime Loyalty Laws for Revenge and Profit* (El Paso, TX: LFB Scholarly Publishers, 2012).

25   The definitive biography of Debs is Nick Salvatore, *Eugene V. Debs: Citizen and Socialist* (Urbana, IL: University of Illinois Press, 2007).

26   See Newton-Matza, *Jazz Age*, Chapter 7.

BIBLIOGRAPHY

Brissenden, Paul. *The IWW: A Study of American Syndicalism*. New York: Russell & Russell, 1919.

Chafee, Zechariah. *Free Speech in the United States*. Cambridge, MA: Harvard University Press, 1948.

Chaplin, Ralph. *Wobbly: The Rough-and-Tumble Story of an American Radical*. Chicago, IL: University of Chicago Press, 1948.

Donalson, Daniel G. *The Espionage and Sedition Acts of World War I: Using Wartime Loyalty Laws for Revenge and Profit*. El Paso, TX: LFB Scholarly Publishers, 2012.

Kazin, Michael. *American Dreamers: How the Left Changed America.* New York: Alfred A. Knopf, 2011.

Kornbluh, Joyce L., *Rebel Voices: An IWW Anthology.* Chicago, IL: Charles H. Kerr, 1988.

McGuckin, Henry E. *Memoirs of a Wobbly.* Chicago, IL: Charles H. Kerr, 1987.

Mereto, Joseph. *The Red Conspiracy.* New York: The National Historical Society, 1920.

Meyer, Howard N. *The Amendment that Refused to Die.* Boston, MA: Beacon Press, 1978.

Newton-Matza, Mitchell. *Intelligent and Honest Radicals: The Chicago Federation of Labor and the Politics of Progression.* Lanham, MD: Lexington Books, 2013.

——, *Jazz Age: People and Perspectives.* Santa Barbara, CA: ABC-CLIO, 2009.

Renshaw, Patrick. *The Wobblies: The Story of Syndicalism in the United States.* New York: Doubleday & Company, 1967.

Salvatore, Nick. *Eugene V. Debs: Citizen and Socialist.* Urbana, IL: University of Illinois Press, 2007. Second edition.

Sinclair, Upton. *Boston.* New York: Albert & Charles Boni, 1928.

CHAPTER 6

Legacies

The Soviet Ark sailed. The IWW was decimated. The Communist Party was underground. People convicted under the Acts were freed. The Italian Anarchists Sacco and Vanzetti were executed for a robbery and murder, in which the evidence was thin at best. John Scopes was convicted for violating a law forbidding the teaching of evolution (the law in which he was convicted was overturned). The country didn't skip a beat. As the oft-quoted phrase by President Calvin Coolidge went: "The business of America is business."

After the post-war economic depression, the economy began to boom. The stock market soared, investments went rampant, and many were rich "on paper." Wild investments became the norm. When not in the stock market, real estate especially became big business. When the Florida land boom ended with a hurricane, people still believed prosperity was just a piece of paper away. But as the so-called "Roaring Twenties" was in full swing, some memories were lost. The country was back to the idea of a stable capitalist country. The memories of those who lost their liberties because of their beliefs were no longer a concern. After all, these people were "un-American" to begin with, so their plight was no longer worth considering. There was easy money to be made. At least so they thought.

The threat of radicalism overturning the country was not as strong as the morality of the nation. With the end of the Victorian Era, and the perceived moral code, people were openly expressing themselves in ways not seen in the mainstream public before.[1] The threat of radicalism overturning the country was not as strong as that of the changing morality of the nation.

Calmer times seem to be the order of the day. But with the onset of the Great Depression, which was worldwide, there were new problems besides those of the economy. Marxist-based radicals would prey upon the crisis to prove their point. Organizing the masses would seem easier than ever. If the business of America was business, this would imply that everyone had an office desk somewhere. But who would produce all this material output? The businessmen? Someone still had to do the actual work. Although the Espionage Act was still valid, the time seemed ripe for a revolution, although most cared about their next meal and not what laws were on the books.

But the near future would challenge the idea of who was an enemy, and who was not. That answer was just as clear in WWI as it was in the 1930s. Germany, soon to be led by Adolph Hitler, was seen as a problem early on. The story of his march towards conquering Europe is the topic of many books and films, and countless documentaries. As with WWI, the Huns were coming. But at this time, Germany was led by a homicidal maniac, and was clearly the aggressor.

However, there was a new unexpected enemy: Asia. Both China and Japan gave reasons to be worried. First, Japan began its full campaign to claim mainland Asia, especially China. There were some confrontations with the U.S., and Japan actually apologized for some actions. Since the Pacific Ocean provided some cushioning, an attack on American soil was not considered likely.

But with Japan's invasion of Manchuria, and then China, there was a new threat looming. China was dealing with decades of civil war. On the Nationalist side, the government was led by General Chiang Kai-shek. In exile was the Chinese Communist Party (CCP) under the leadership of Mao Zedong. While the two sides united to fight the Japanese, when WWII was over, the civil war again went into full swing. When the Communists took control on October 1, 1949, there was now another Marxist-based country. When China and the Soviet Union seemed to combine ideological forces (not to mention the Soviets provided military training to the Chinese), there was even more cause to worry, although the U.S. did not realize at first there was not much love between the two countries. And, when combined with the French battling against the freedom fighters in Vietnam, led by the Communist Ho Chi Minh, the intensity continued (discussed further below).

The United States had to make a most unlikely alliance—with the Soviet Union. The Russians had a long-standing feud with Japan, having lost to them in the Russo-Japanese War of 1905. Making an alliance, however shaky, with a potential ally seemed to make sense. The United States finally recognized the Soviet Union in 1935. The U.S. government wanted to make it clear the Soviet Union propaganda campaigns would cease.

While the alliance between the U.S. and the Soviet Union was one of convenience, when WWII ended, the Cold War began, as did another Red Scare (to be discussed below). During the war, there was a mutual distrust, as is well known. The United States kept the Soviets from knowing about the atomic bomb until the last moment, as they did with any other technological advancements. In the 1983 film *The Right Stuff*, based upon the Tom Wolfe novel, when Chuck Yeager broke the sound barrier, a reporter wanted to make it a story. A military officer stopped the call, making it clear they did not want the Soviets to know. The reporter exclaimed "But they're our allies!" The marriage of convenience was quickly in divorce.

With the threat of another world war, and having to work with the Soviets, the notion that Communists posed a serious threat re-emerged with a vigor not seen since the Palmer Raids. Besides the notion that the Soviets were attempting to infiltrate the country through the now-united Communist Party, the labor movement was making strides never seen before. President Franklin D. Roosevelt's (FDR) New Deal programs, designed to combat the Great Depression, included reaching out to the labor movement as a way of both stabilizing the marketplace and keeping a steady, placated workforce.

The AFL was still going strong. However, it faced competition from a new, growing organization: the Committee of Industrial Organizations (later becoming the Congress of Industrial Organizations—CIO), led by John L. Lewis, who first brought the idea of this group in 1928. The AFL was criticized for years by many portions of the labor movement for being a craft union, meaning one had to have a specific skill to be organized. Lewis, among many others, argued for industrial unionism, meaning any worker was eligible for union membership. But what made the CIO suspect at first was their use of Communists, who had excellent organization skills. Despite Lewis' assertion that the CIO was not a Communist organization, their very presence made them suspect. In 1955 the two groups united to form what is now known as the AFL–CIO, a group strong into contemporary times.[2]

WWII had its official start on September 1, 1939, although the U.S. was not yet militarily involved. Despite the fairly recent recognition of the Soviet Union, the nation continued to use legal means to control radicalism. One such measure was the Alien Registration Act of 1940, usually referred to as the Smith Act.[3] In a measure similar to the mass deportations of alien residents during the Palmer Raids era, this law also addressed immigration. The law required the fingerprinting of all aliens entering the U.S., and strengthened existing laws governing the admission and deportation of such aliens.

However, the Smith Act is known more for the government's continued attacks on radicalism, particularly Marxist-based groups. The government deemed it unlawful for any person to advocate or teach the overthrow or destruction of any government in the U.S. by violence or any other type of force. Moreover, it also became illegal to organize or become a member of any group dedicated to teaching any doctrines that follow this line.

The usual arguments concerning this law were put forward—free speech, patriotism, and the threat of any internal dangers in the face of an ever-growing global crisis. The notion of maintaining a stable home front was once again in the fore. And so were the expected legal challenges to the Smith Act.

Among others throughout the free speech battles, three certain U.S. Supreme Court cases resulted in decisions that paired so well with those during the First Red Scare: *Eugene Dennis, et al. v. United States* (1951), *Pennsylvania v. Nelson* (1956), and *Yates v. United States* (1957). Whether or not these cases were consistent with prior decisions (and the U.S. Supreme Court has overturned itself on numerous occasions), the precedents set during the WWI era remained.

The most famous of all the post-WWII Supreme Court cases involving the Smith Act was *Dennis*. Eugene Dennis (1905–1961) will probably be remembered as the most prominent of all American Communists in the post-WWII years.

Dennis was born Francis Xavier Waldron in 1905, which, coincidentally, is the same year the Industrial Workers of the World (IWW) was founded, a group he later joined as an organizer. At one point in 1929 he fled to the Soviet Union in response to his possible indictment in California's syndicalism laws. Upon his return in 1935, he would be known as Eugene Dennis. With the onset of the Cold War upon WWII's conclusion, Dennis' support and alliance with the Soviet Union would cause him innumerable problems, especially when he became General Secretary of the CPUSA. He never masked his allegiance with Moscow's policies.

In total, Dennis and 10 others were brought up on charges under the Smith Act (one of the defendants, William Z. Foster, another well-known Communist, was not prosecuted because of ill health). Despite the fact the defendants claimed freedom of speech, and they were not actively overthrowing the U.S. government, the trial proceeded in 1949, which would last until October of that same year—when, like the trial of *The Masses*, it was not a good time to be a radical.

The issue at hand was whether the defendants were actually trying to overthrow the U.S. government. But, under the prosecutor John McGohey, while the defendants did not explicitly advocate a violent revolution in the country, the fact they subscribed to Marxist-based ideology that called for such action, was cause enough for conviction (referring back to the Merritt Conspiracy Laws of Illinois—See Chapter 1). Many believed the trial was an excuse to promote Communist ideology. The trial ended in October, with guilty verdicts for all. Besides a 5-year prison sentence, a hefty fine was also imposed.

The case went through numerous appeals, eventually winding up in the U.S. Supreme Court as *Dennis v. United States*.[4] In a 6–2 decision, the

Supreme Court upheld the Smith Act (one of the justices, Tom C. Clark, did not participate as he was Attorney General when the case was first brought up). In an opinion delivered by Chief Justice Fred M. Vinson, with several concurring opinions written by justices such as Felix Frankfurter. In the opinion, society has interests, but the fear of Communist ideology/reality made the case fall within the law. Prior to the *Dennis* case, the courts tended to hold that an ideological argument could not be limitable.

The minority dissenting opinions were rather clearer on the issue. Justice Hugo Black vigorously argued that the 11 men only agreed to assemble, publish, and talk of opinions. There were no charges that they were actually conspiring to commit any overt acts to overthrow the government, and that the case was unconstitutional as it involved censorship. They were discussing doctrine, and thus were within their First Amendment rights.

The next major decision involving the Smith Act was the 1956 case *Pennsylvania v. Nelson.*[5] Many states passed laws requiring individuals in government employment to take an oath stating they were not, nor have been, in the Communist Party. This was also required of public school teachers, garbage collectors, and anyone else having dealings with the government. From 1951–1954, the Supreme Court upheld the constitutionality of such laws. The shift began in the mid-1950s, especially with the *Nelson* case.

Steve Nelson was convicted under Pennsylvania's Sedition Act, part of which required members of the Communist Party to be denied jobs. Nelson was convicted, sentenced to 20 years in prison, and fined $10,000 plus $13,000 to cover the conviction costs. Nelson, however, argued that the Smith Act—although written after the Pennsylvania law—preempted his conviction.

The Supreme Court ruled 6–3 in favor of Nelson. However, the decision was not on any substantial question, but on technical grounds. Writing the opinion of the court, Chief Justice Earl Warren held that federal law is preeminent, and that Pennsylvania was getting into the federal area of jurisdiction, although the states were free to defend themselves. In the absence of any federal legislation addressing any specific topics, the states were free to act. However, federal legislation did exist, and the conviction was set aside.

The third decision to address the Smith Act was the 1957 case *Yates v. United States.*[6] In this case, 14 individuals, considered "second string Communists," were convicted under the Smith Act. Similar to the *Dennis* case, those convicted argued they were merely engaged in ideological discussion and not planning an actual conspiracy to overthrow the government.

The Supreme Court agreed with these arguments and overturned the convictions by a 6–1 vote. In writing for the majority, Justice John Marshall

Harlan held that these people were only members of the conspiracy and not organizers, and that advocacy to do something was one issue, but advocating to believe in something was another. This decision did not overturn the Smith Act, and it still recognized the right for society to protect itself, but the power of the Act was all but diminished.

It is not difficult to see how such cases arose with the Cold War in full swing. The most prominent strikes against radicalism came with the House of Un-American Activities Committee (HUAC) and McCarthyism, under U.S. Senator Joseph McCarthy. While these stories are well told, it bears mentioning in light of the Acts and the aftermath.

What worried many Americans was how the Soviet Union would try to spread its influence in the United States. Since the Soviet Union exploded its own atomic bomb in 1949, that fear intensified. First, how did the Soviets catch up to the U.S. so quickly with such atomic energy (leading to spy ring speculations)? And, more importantly, was the idea of the Soviets "boring from within," meaning a military strike was not necessary, and infiltrating the country clandestinely through disguised agents, who would then slowly indoctrinate the population, especially impressionable youth.

But this begs a bigger question: What exactly does a Communist/radical look like? Unless one is walking down the street wearing clearly marked apparel, or carrying an explicitly worded sign, how can anyone tell who is a Soviet agent/sympathizer? Are they tall, short, skinny, large, hairy, bald, or a certain race? (this last point to be discussed below). A Soviet cadre attempting to establish a Communist cell, with the hopes of it spreading, will do so slowly and carefully so as not to arouse suspicion. By slowly changing the minds of the American populace, the Soviet Union could more easily take over.

The first, and foremost, government strike against radicalism during the Cold War, especially Communism, was with the House Committee on Un-American Activities (HUAC), which was created in 1938 as a temporary committee, with Martin Dies as its first chairman. Considering the times, one of its primary focuses was against potential Nazi activities within the U.S. But HUAC came to represent more fear than the idea of protecting the country against Nazis. HUAC will be remembered as a symbol of the violation of civil liberties.

The answer remains: what is/was an "un-American" activity? Left-wing radical groups were of course a main target. With WWII looming in 1938 (although some years before American direct involvement), Nazis were certainly a growing enemy. But many people wondered why groups like the Mafia and the Ku Klux Klan (KKK) were not investigated. Members of those two groups would argue they were very much true Americans. They upheld capitalism, promoted family values (whatever those might have been), and, more importantly, did not threaten to overturn the government. If anything, they claimed they were participating in what was considered mainstream American society.[7]

As mentioned earlier, the CIO was under suspicion. Dies wanted to investigate this union organization, then a mere 2 years old. John Frey of the American Federation of Labor (AFL) was called to testify before HUAC. At the time, the AFL was essentially battling the CIO. Dies opened the hearing but not wanting a witch hunt or character assassination. Frey, in foreshadowing Senator Joseph McCarthy, presented a list of 300 names of what he called card-carrying Communists.

Frey was followed by Walter Steele, an ultra-patriotic person. Steele presented a list of what he considered to be un-American groups. In what shocked many, both the Boy and Girl Scouts were on this list. To Steele, the reasoning was that these were international organizations, and could thus be infiltrated. Child film star Shirley Temple's name once appeared on a masthead of a committee that was on Steele's list. Members of President Franklin D. Roosevelt's (FDR) cabinet were furious, and it was heard to be said (to paraphrase), "why not raid her dollhouse?"

When testifying before HUAC, accused persons could not defend themselves in ways accorded in a court of law. In some cases, the accused had to print a retraction against the charges in a newspaper's obituary column. Especially in the case of Frey testifying against the CIO, libel and slander laws could not be applied. However, any witnesses could invoke the Fifth Amendment against self-incrimination.

In the late 1940s, HUAC turned its attention to Hollywood, which was considered to be a haven for radicals, especially Communists. While this sentiment was brewing for some time, in October 1947, HUAC subpoenaed people in Hollywood. These can easily be discerned as two groups, the "friendly" and the "unfriendly" witnesses. The main friendly witnesses were Walt Disney, future Republican U.S. president Ronald Reagan (who was then president of the Screen Actor's Guild), and actor Adolph Menjou. All testified about the presence of Communists in Hollywood and how they constituted a threat.

In all, 43 people were called as witnesses, of which 19 refused to participate. Of these, 10 would eventually be known as the "Hollywood Ten," and part of the unfriendly witnesses. Writer John Lawson testified first. In accordance with Committee practices, witnesses were allowed to read an opening statement. Lawson began by blasting HUAC, accusing them of conducting illegal trials, and it was wrong that they could not face their accusers. Furthermore, HUAC was simply harassing him, and others, merely for their opinions. Lawson did not invoke his Fifth Amendment rights, got into a shouting match with HUAC, was escorted out, and eventually cited for contempt of Congress.

Novelist and screenwriter Dalton Trumbo would never admit to being a member of the Communist Party during the 1930s, and was also cited for contempt. Screenwriter Ring Lardner, Jr., felt he could joke his way through the hearings, only to find out HUAC had no sense of humor, and was also cited. With HUAC, if one was a former Communist and now a good flag-waving patriot, all was forgiven. What the Committee especially wanted to know was with whom did they associate. Such testimony was not protected by the Fifth Amendment. The refusal to name names cost many their entertainment careers.[8]

All top 50 Hollywood producers unanimously agreed never to hire the Hollywood Ten until they had cleared their names. Many people and careers were ruined, and some, like Trumbo and Lardner, worked under assumed names. Lardner would win the Academy Award for Best Adapted Screenplay for his work on the 1970 film *M*A*S*H* (based upon the novel by Richard Hooker). Trumbo wrote the screenplay for the Kirk Douglas 1960 film *Spartacus*, which had strong patriotic tones, something Douglas would later reveal. However, many were not so lucky.

Hunting Communists, or radicals of any kind, became big business, and very competitive. Besides the government actively persecuting radicals, private groups did as well. The most notorious of such groups was AWARE, created by American Business Consultants (ABC) in 1953. While formed by three ex-FBI agents who felt agency director J. Edgar Hoover was not doing enough to pursue Communists, it was Lawrence Johnson and Vincent Hartnett who essentially ran the show. They were guided at first by the anonymously written 1950 book *Red Channels* about how Communists had infiltrated Hollywood and the media, which cited many names.

It seemed few, if any, were exempt from their wrath. Philip Loeb was the star of what many called television's first situation comedy, *The Goldbergs* (running 1959–1956), a show about a Jewish family. Loeb's name was in *Red Channels*, and in 1950 General Foods, the show's sponsor, wanted him off the program. This demand was refused, and General Foods withdrew its sponsorship.[9] The show was canceled only to re-emerge in 1952, only without Loeb. The original demand was met. With Harnett working in the background, it got to the point where he could not get any sort of job, despite his insistence he was never a Communist. Depression set in and Loeb committed suicide by an overdose in a hotel room in 1955.

What helped Hartnett and Johnson was their standing in their prospective communities. Hartnett was behind promoting *Red Channels*, and Johnson was influential in business circles. Johnson encouraged store displays to create a boycott of products by companies who sponsored shows featuring supposed Communists. Rival products by good American companies would receive their own signs promoting not just their product(s) but their patriotism.

AWARE's 1962 downfall came for two reasons: The end of McCarthyism and blacklisting, and the case of John Henry Faulk. A radio personality and storyteller with a laid back style, AWARE went after Faulk. When he eventually lost his radio job, AWARE did all it could to keep him unemployed. Inspired by fellow media personality and anti-blacklisting champion Edward R. Murrow, Faulk filed suit in 1957. Although opponents of the suit, including anti-Communist attorney Roy Cohn, managed to delay the trial for 5 years, in 1962 a jury found in Faulk's favor.

Johnson and Hartnett were called to the stand, and completely fell apart. Hartnett admitted to blacklisting a man because he wore a red Santa Claus suit. Johnson did worse, and died before the trial was over. The award settlement was $3.5 million, even more than originally asked for. The award was later reduced to a half million dollars, with Faulk eventually winding up with $75,000.

Perhaps the person who most defined the early Cold War anti-Communist era was none other than Senator Joseph McCarthy (1908–1957) from Wisconsin. In a story already well told, documented, and debated, it still remains important to briefly discuss the era that bears his name: McCarthyism. First elected to the Senate over political powerhouse Robert La Follette in 1946, his first years in office were lackluster at best. Like other politicians on the hot seat, he needed an issue to propel his name forward. Communism was the answer.

On February 9, 1950, McCarthy gave one of the most remembered—and notorious—speeches ever made by a politician. Speaking in Wheeling, West Virginia, McCarthy claimed to have a list of 205 names of Communists working in the U.S. State Department (although later he said the number was 57). After some further background checks on State Department employees, the Senate created the Tydings Committee, headed up by Millard Tydings, to investigate. Having a Democratic majority (McCarthy was Republican), the committee found no credence in McCarthy's claims. Yet, as long as McCarthy continued any attacks on the Senate floor, according to the Constitution, he was safe from any and all libel and slander suits.

McCarthy also made the military suspect, as well as the homosexual community. However, with all the hysteria on both sides of the issue, on December 2, 1954, the Senate voted to censure McCarthy. With his reputation and political career now in shambles, McCarthy died on May 2, 1957, at the age of 48. He still remains a controversial figure, and the George Clooney-directed 2005 film *Good Night, and Good Luck* shows how Edward R. Murrow and others used the media to counter-attack McCarthy's claims.[10]

As this author points out in a previous work: "Studies of anti-Communist activities during this time tend to center around Senator Joe McCarthy, a name generally associated with lies, exaggeration and intolerance." Recent scholarship suggests that McCarthy has been unjustly vilified, his actions misrepresented or outright fabricated and that he had actual proof of Communists working in the federal government.[11] In M. Stanton Evans' *Blacklisted by History*, several high profile government employees, and their alleged activities, gave credence to his accusations. Evans was able to utilize recently declassified documents as well as re-examining prior scholarship and reports."[12]

Other world events gave rise to fear of takeover of the United States by Marxist-based countries or conflicts. The Communist takeover of China in 1949, and the subsequent "friendship" with the Soviet Union seemed threatening enough. But the conflicts in Korea and Vietnam gave a new spin on the Cold War, and, thus, the fear of a radical takeover.

The U.S. involvement of the Korean War in the early 1950s, followed by a slow involvement into the Vietnam situation later that decade can both easily be classified as part of the Cold War. In both instances, the two Asian countries were divided between north and south battling for supremacy; the north being Communist, with democratic forces in the south. Also, in both instances, each side was supported in numerous ways by their allies. North Korea gained a valuable enemy when the Chinese entered the conflict on behalf of their Communist brethren, along with Soviet supplied weapons. The same goes for South Korea with not just the United States, but also the United Nations joining in. Vietnam experienced a similar situation, although later in that conflict strong American anti-war sentiment is still remembered as a vital part of the 1960s.

As opposed to spotting a Soviet, the Americans figured to have an easier time identifying an Asian Communist (or, at least they thought as much). Using racial stereotypes, an Asian could easily be detained and questioned, if not detained, under suspicion of their being a Communist or Communist sympathizer. Establishing a foothold with white America would be much more difficult than that of a Soviet.

Backlash against radicals, especially Communists, remains part of popular culture. In returning to a focus on Hollywood, filmmaker Elia Kazan (1909–2003), one of HUAC's "friendly" witnesses testified before the committee. During the mid-1930s, Kazan was a member of the American Communist Party, although for just under 2 years. When HUAC approached Kazan in April 1952, to testify, he had first refused to provide names of fellow group members, especially those in the entertainment business. He eventually provided the information HUAC demanded. Many of those identified wound up losing their careers, and Kazan was shunned by many in the film industry.

Kazan would later claim he felt betrayed by the Communist movement, and did not feel he should surrender his own career to protect his former comrades. It is argued that his 1954 film *On the Waterfront*, which dealt with the exposing of corruption in the unions, was his explanation for why he took such a stand before HUAC. In 1999 Kazan won the Lifetime Achievement award during the annual Academy Award presentation show. While many stood up and applauded Kazan for his contributions to art, many refused to stand, much less applaud. While Kazan is not as well remembered in contemporary times, parts of his legacy are still debated.[13]

Television also took part in examining radicals. One of the first (if not the first) shows to have parables about radicalism and the Cold War was the initial run of the classic *Twilight Zone*. Some of the episodes dealt with the potential threat of nuclear warfare, while another, using the analogy of an alien invasion, was a thinly disguised look at how people feared Communist infiltration.

The famous long-running television show M★A★S★H (based upon the film mentioned above) addressed the situation Kazan faced in the 1979 episode "Are You Now, Margaret?"[14] As known, the show takes place in the early 1950s during the Korean War. The character of Major Margaret "Hot Lips" Hoolihan, is a dedicated, extremely loyal and patriotic American. A congressional aide shows up one day and eventually accuses her of being a Communist sympathizer, all because an old college boyfriend was placed on a list of subversives. The idea of Hoolihan being a sympathizer is ridiculous, but if she provides the aide with a list of their college companions he could go easy on her. Regardless of whatever cooperation she provides, or denies, her reputation would be ruined and she would lose her commission. But, since this show was a situation comedy, her friends help her out in a comedic way to blackmail the aide into leaving her alone. Still, the episode aptly demonstrates what many innocent people had to face during the 1950s.

Starting in the 1980s, the portrayal of Communists—both foreign and domestic—had some differing views, although for the most part these radicals were still dangerous and needed to be exterminated. Warren Beatty's 1981 film *Reds*, however, took a more sympathetic view of radicals. The film is a biopic of John Reed, an American journalist whose witnessing of the 1917 Bolshevik Revolution in Russia resulted in the famous book *Ten Days that Shook the World*. Beatty shows the human side of the radical movement, and how they had thoughts and feelings as anyone else. While winning four Academy Awards, it was a failure at the box office. That the film was almost 4 hours long could be one reason, with another being that since the Cold War was still going on, making such a film about radicals was still controversial.

Other films in the 1980s dealt with the Cold War. Sylvester Stallone's *Rambo* series dealt more with Vietnam than anything (itself, as mentioned, as part of the Cold War), but it was his 1985 film *Rocky IV*, that especially promoted ultra-patriotism. As part of the popular *Rocky* series, this particular episode had professional boxer Rocky going head-to-head with a massive Soviet opponent in a Russian boxing ring. Not only does Rocky win the fight, but he also wins over the hearts of the Russian spectators. It was a "demonstration" of how one good American alone can defeat an entire ideology.

Martial arts expert Chuck Norris contributed to his share of what many would argue are propaganda films. His 1985 *Invasion U.S.A.* had Norris as a one-man army stopping an invasion. His *Missing in Action* films, like those of Stallone's, also dealt with Vietnam, and how easy it could be to defeat those lousy, pesky Commies.

Probably the one film that especially demonstrated the fighting American spirit against Communists was the 1984 *Red Dawn* (remade in 2012). When a Communist invasion hits a small town, it is up to the high school students, especially the football team, to fight in this country's defense. The first version still has somewhat of a cult status, especially with those who grew up in the 1980s. The second version, however, was vilified for its implausible premise. While it was still about an invasion, incorporating the current tensions with North Korea was laughable. A Soviet invasion, no matter how small, could be at least minimally believable, but could a country as small as North Korea ever possibly invade the United States?

In contemporary times, a new kind of radicalism grabbed the nation's attention, and its fears. Marxist-based groups such as Communists and Anarchists were no longer considered to be a danger to the country. The threats were both foreign and domestic, but in a way not previously expected. Despite the fact that the Espionage Act was still on the books, although watered down by court decisions, no legislation could prepare for the years of turmoil that started in the 1990s.

Domestically, there were two unrelated but yet equally shattering events. The first took place at the Branch Davidian compound in Waco, Texas. In a ranch occupied by a religious cult led by David Koresh, there were reports of weapons and ammunition being stockpiled, all illegal. The U.S. Bureau of Alcohol, Tobacco, and Firearms (ATF), attempted to search the premises for the munitions on February 28, 1993. Koresh had prior warning to the raid, and a gun battle ensured.

ATF, along with the Federal Bureau of Investigation (FBI) would surround the compound, resulting in an extended standoff. On April 19, tear gas was used, and, for unknown reasons, fires broke out. Approximately 74 people were killed (including Koresh), and 15 wounded. Despite the controversial nature of this cult, many wondered if their threat warranted such an attack. Defenders of the raid pointed to the dangerous nature of the cult, including the sexual exploitation of children.[15]

The most devastating domestic terrorist attack occurred on April 19, 1995, with the Oklahoma City Bombing. A car bomb was detonated outside the Alfred P. Murrah Federal Building at 9:02 a.m., killing 168 people, including children in a daycare inside the building. Carried out by former U.S. Army sergeant Timothy McVeigh, aided in the planning by Terry and James Nichols, and Michael Fortier (who later cooperated with authorities), the attack was inspired by the book *The Turner Diaries* by Andrew McDonald (the pseudonym of William Luther Pierce). Called "the Bible of the racist right," the book describes a similar attack on a federal building. All conspirators were captured, and McVeigh, at his request, would be executed. The others received prison sentences.[16]

The fear of domestic enemies shifted from the left to the right. While the FBI still kept an eye on left-wing groups such as Communists, that group was no longer considered to be a threat. Right-wing paramilitary groups were monitored with even more vigor. Rap and Hip-Hop artists who performed songs with violent and/or other controversial topics were being considered as a threat to American society.

But America was not prepared for the events of September 11, 2001. On that infamous day, the worst terrorist attack on American soil occurred, resulting in thousands of deaths. Nineteen radical Islamic terrorists, backed by the extremist group al-Qaeda, hijacked four commercial airliners in the morning hours. Two of the airliners crashed into the two towers of the World Trade Center in New York City, both of which would eventually collapse. One crashed into the west side of the Pentagon in Washington, DC. On the fourth, the passengers learned of the other planes and fought their attackers. That plane would crash into a field in Pennsylvania.

Outrage filled not just the nation but the entire world. President George W. Bush would use the attacks as a means to go into a war with Afghanistan (where al-Qaeda leader Osama bin Laden was said to be hiding), and a second war with Iraq. However, many people compared 9/11 with the 1941 Japanese attack on Pearl Harbor. Besides both being surprise attacks, many wondered if the U.S. government had prior knowledge of the attack as a justification for war.[17] The government would pass the USA Patriot Act of 2001 (hereinafter Patriot Act), signed by President George W. Bush, which gave the government additional powers to combat terrorism.[18] But, as for the Acts, how far can the government go to protect the country, and how would this affect civil liberties? The debate rages on.

Many comparisons can be made between the Acts and the Patriot Act. Both dealt with the country in a time of fear and paranoia. Briefly, provisions of the Patriot Act provided numerous means to combat terrorism, as stated above. Such powers involved increased surveillance procedures, preventing money laundering, improving intelligence and information collections practices, and giving increased powers to investigate potential terrorist threats.

There are numerous comparisons between this legislation and those during WWI. As with the Acts, many felt the Patriot Act trampled on civil liberties. Others were uncomfortable with the sweeping expansion of government powers, including the right to check one's library records. Many also felt that specific members of society were being targeted; the Germans during WWI, and those of the Middle East following the attacks of 9/11. Names of certain items were also changed, just like in WWI. Since France refused to cooperate with the wars in the Middle East, in the Capitol Building cafeteria "French Fries" was changed to "Freedom Fries," just as many German names for products were made more Anglican during WWI.

But one difference stands out. Whereas in WWI it was often difficult to spot a potential German spy due to their European appearance, those from the Middle East were far easier to target. There were many reports from those who reported being detained merely due to their Arab appearance (forgetting that not everyone from the Middle East was Arab). More than one airline passenger was escorted off a plane for further scrutiny because another passenger felt uncomfortable to be traveling with a potential terrorist, even if that person was born and bred in the United States.

Some years later, another radical Islamic group, ISIS, threatened further attacks against Western nations, especially the United States. There were other instances of bombing attacks in the country, such as the Boston Marathon Bombing of 2013. Also in 2013, Edward Snowden leaked thousands of classified documents to the media in order to, in his opinion, let the public know what was going on in the upper echelons of the government. A former employee of the Central Intelligence Agency (CIA) and contractor with the National Security Agency (NSA), Snowden would find asylum in Russia (where he still resides at the time of this writing). Some call him a traitor for betraying government secrets, while others consider him a hero for exposing what truly happens in the government.

Starting with WWI all the way into the twenty-first century, the fear of internal dissent and violence kept growing. On June 12, 2016, a New York-born Omar Mateen, of Afghani descent, opened fire at the Pulse dance club in Orlando, Florida (at the time of this writing the death toll was at 49, with wounded at 53). While born in America, his radicalization became a hot topic throughout the media. In WWI people were afraid of not just German sympathizers but the influence of Marxist-based groups on the population. Now there was a new fear, a new way of "boring from within."

At the risk of reiterating the first chapter, one final look at some of the past historiography bears another mention. Again, Stephen Kohn in *American Political Prisoners* believes that during the WWI era "a developing human rights movement was uprooted and disposed of in an unmarked grave."[19] Some would argue that the Patriot Act in the aftermath of 9/11 was doing the exact same thing by overly intruding into the private lives of American citizens. Paul L. Murphy in *World War I and the Origin of Civil Liberties in the United States* agrees with this when he says the treatment of civil liberties during WWI was new and disturbing.[20] But as Robert Justin Goldstein reflects into modern times, "the severe governmental repression which developed did not constitute an irrational response."[21] In the wake of the Branch Davidian raid, Oklahoma City Bombing, and 9/11, many would agree with this assessment.

Since 9/11, and the growing threat of ISIS, determining an enemy, real or perceived, took on qualities echoing the WWI years. In contemporary times it is the Islamic community and its sympathizers. Joan M. Jensen's *The Price of Vigilance* also pointed this out by discussing groups who were seen to be targeting any German threat to the well-being of the nation during WWI.[22] Donald G. Donalson's *The Espionage and Sedition Acts of World War I: Using Wartime Loyalty for Revenge and Profit* also discusses this by examining how people used the Acts for personal gain by targeting anyone they felt could even be remotely suspicious of un-American activities.[23] Although more cultural sensitivities currently prevail in mainstream entertainment, for years Hollywood used racial and ethnic stereotypes to clearly define an enemy, all for the sake of selling tickets.

Christopher Capozzola's *Uncle Sam Wants You: World War I and the Making of the Modern American Citizen* particularly examines the notion of patriotism. Beginning with the now-iconic symbol of the Uncle Sam character saying "I want YOU," Capozzola argues "When Uncle Sam jabbed his finger at the American public, he pointed out their rights, and he also pointed out who was or who wasn't an American."[24] When Geoffrey Stone writes in *Perilous Times: Free Speech in Wartime*, he states "The enemy is more likely to fight fiercely if it is confident and believes its adversary divided and uncertain."[25] Opposition to the wars in Afghanistan and Iraq, as well as Americans attempting to join ISIS, was beneficial to the Jihadist belief they were doing the right thing by attacking the decadent West.[26] During WWI, and WWII, these sentiments were also felt by the patriotic public, who wanted dissenters suppressed in order to prevent any additional strife.

The ability to command the loyalty of citizens is one of the most perplexing problems facing the modern state. If Senator Julius Kahn had his way, a lot of rope would be used to silence many, many voices. If the Acts of WWI shows anything, they show the resolve of people to exercise their constitutional rights, no matter what the consequences may be. Once again, WWI became not just a battle between armies, but also between minds.

NOTES

1   For more information about the cultural history of the 1920s, see Mitchell Newton-Matza, Ed., *Jazz Age: People and Perspectives* (Santa Barbara, CA: ABC–CLIO, 2009).

2   For an excellent look at the Communist involvement in the Alabama labor movement, see Robin D.G. Kelley's *Hammer and Hoe* (Chapel Hill, NC: University of North Carolina Press, 1990).

3   *Alien Registration Act*, Pub. L. 76–670, 54 Stat. 670, 1940.

4   *Dennis v. United States*, 341 U.S. 494.

5   *Pennsylvania v. Nelson*, 350 U.S. 497.

6   *Yates v. United States*, 354 U.S. 298.

7   By no means is this to be construed that the author is defending the activities of either group. The point is merely that these groups believed they were true and better Americans than any radical group.

8   There are many good sources regarding HUAC and Hollywood. Especially see Norma Barzman, *The Red and the Blacklist: The Intimate Memoir of a Hollywood Expatriate* (New York: Thunder's Mouth/Nation Books, 2004); Paul Buhle and David Wagner, *Blacklisted: The Film Lover's Guide to the Hollywood Blacklist* (New York: Palgrave Macmillan, 2003); and Bernard F. Dick, *Radical Innocence: A Critical Study of the Hollywood Ten* (Lexington, KS: University Press of Kentucky, 1989).

9   In the early days of television one single company would sponsor a show, as opposed to contemporary times when commercials from numerous companies provided sponsorship.

10 For further reading, see Ellen Schrecker, *Many Are the Crimes: McCarthyism in America* (Boston, MA: Little, Brown, 1998); Arthur Herman, *Joseph McCarthy: Reexamining the Life and Legacy of America's Most Hated Senator* (New York: Free Press, 1999); Richard M. Fried, *Nightmare in Red: The McCarthy Era in Perspective* (Oxford, UK: Oxford University Press, 1990).

11 See M. Stanton Evans, *Blacklisted by History: The Untold Story of Senator Joe McCarthy and his Fight Against America's Enemies* (New York: Crown Forum, 1997).

12 Mitchell Newton-Matza, *Was Domestic Communism an Actual Threat to the U.S. in the Mid-20th Century?* (Santa Barbara, CA: ABC-CLIO, 2011). Also See Evans, 1997.

13 For further reading, see Richard Schickel, *Elia Kazan: A Biography* (New York: HarperCollins, 2005).

14 "Are You Now, Margaret?," *M*A*S*H*, aired 24 September 1979.

15 Charles Louis Richter, "Waco, Texas, Tragedy," in Disasters and Tragic Events: An Encyclopedia of Catastrophes in American History. (Santa Barbara, CA: ABC–CLIO, 2014), 554–558.

16 See Cord Scott, "Oklahoma City Bombing," in *Disasters and Tragic Events: An Encyclopedia of Catastrophes in American History* (Santa Barbara, CA: ABC-CLIO, 2014), 562–565.

17   See William A. Taylor, "Terrorist Attacks of 9/11," in *Disasters and Tragic Events: An Encyclopedia of Catastrophes in American History* (Santa Barbara, CA: ABC-CLIO, 2014), 581–585.

18   *USA Patriot Act*, 115 Stat. 272 (2001).

19   Stephen M. Kohn, *American Political Prisoners* (Westport, CT: Praeger, 1994), 1.

20   Paul L. Murphy, *World War I and the Origin of Civil Liberties in the United States* (New York: W.W. Norton, 1979).

21   Robert Justin Goldstein, *Political Repression in Modern America: 1870s to the Present* (Cambridge, MA: Schenkman, 1978), 107.

22   Joan M. Jensen, *The Price of Vigilance* (Chicago, IL: Rand McNally, 1968).

23   Daniel G. Donalson, *The Espionage and Sedition Acts of World War I: Using Wartime Loyalty Law for Revenge and Profit* (El Paso, TX: LFB Scholarly, 2012).

24   Christopher Capozzola, *Uncle Sam Wants You: World War I and the Making of the Modern American Citizen* (Oxford, UK: Oxford University Press, 2008), 7.

25   Geoffrey R. Stone, *Perilous Times: Free Speech in Wartime* (New York: W.W. Norton, 2004), 4.

26   *Jihad* is actually a misunderstood word. It literally means "struggle." There were two struggles, the greater and the lesser. The greater jihad is similar to the Christian Perfect Act of Contrition, and that is avoid evil and do good. The lesser is what many call "holy war" whereby a Muslim is expected to lay down his life in defense of the faith.

BIBLIOGRAPHY

"Are You Now, Margaret?," *M*A*S*H*, aired September 24, 1979.

Barzman, Norma. *The Red and the Blacklist: The Intimate Memoir of a Hollywood Expatriate.* New York: Thunder's Mouth/Nation Books, 2004.

Buhle, Paul and David Wagner. *Blacklisted: The Film Lover's Guide to the Hollywood Blacklist.* New York: Palgrave Macmillan, 2003.

Capozzola, Christopher. *Uncle Sam Wants You: World War I and the Making of Modern American Citizens.* Oxford: Oxford University Press, 2008.

Dennis v. United States. 341 U.S. 494.

Dick, Bernard F. *Radical Innocence: A Critical Study of the Hollywood Ten.* Lexington, KS: University Press of Kentucky, 1989.

Donalson, Daniel G. *The Espionage and Sedition Acts of World War I: Using Wartime Loyalty Laws for Revenge and Profit.* El Paso, TX: LFB Scholarly Publishers, 2012.

Evans, M. Stanton. *Blacklisted by History: The Untold Story of Senator Joe McCarthy and his Fight Against America's Enemies.* New York: Crown Forum, 1997.

Fried, Richard M. *Nightmare in Red: The McCarthy Era in Perspective.* Oxford, UK: Oxford University Press, 1990.

Goldstein, Robert Justin. *Political Repression in Modern America: 1870 to the Present.* Cambridge, MA: Schenkman, 1978.

Herman, Arthur. *Joseph McCarthy: Reexamining the Life and Legacy of America's Most Hated Senator.* New York: Free Press, 1999.

Jensen, Joan M. *The Price of Vigilance.* Chicago, IL: Rand McNally, 1968.

Kelley, Robin D.G. *Hammer and Hoe.* Chapel Hill, NC: University of North Carolina Press, 1990.

Kohn, Stephen M. *American Political Prisoners*. Westport, CT: Praeger, 1994.

Murphy, Paul L. *World War I: The Origin of Civil Liberties in the United States*. New York: W.W. Norton, 1979.

Newton-Matza, Mitchell, Ed. *Jazz Age: People and Perspectives*. Santa Barbara, CA: ABC-CLIO, 2009.

———. *Was Domestic Communism an Actual Threat to the U.S. in the Mid-20th Century?* Santa Barbara, CA: ABC-CLIO, 2011.

Pennsylvania v. Nelson. 350 U.S. 497.

Rabban, David M. *Free Speech in its Forgotten Years*. Cambridge, UK: Cambridge University Press, 1997.

Richter, Charles Louis "Waco, Texas, Tragedy," in Disasters and Tragic Events: An Encyclopedia of Catastrophes in American History. (Santa Barbara, CA: ABC-CLIO, 2014), 554–558.

Schickel, Richard. *Elia Kazan: A Biography*. New York: HarperCollins, 2005.

Schrecker, Ellen. *Many Are the Crimes: McCarthyism in America*. Boston, MA: Little, Brown, 1998.

Scott, Cord. "Oklahoma City Bombing." *Disasters and Tragic Events: An Encyclopedia of Catastrophes in American History, 562–565*. Santa Barbara, CA: ABC-CLIO, 2014.

Sedition Act, Pub. L. 65–150, 40 Stat. 553, 1918.

Stone, Geoffrey R. *Perilous Times: Free Speech in Wartime*. New York: W.W. Norton, 2004.

Yates v. United States. 354 U.S. 298.

Taylor, William A. *"Terrorist Attacks of 9/11." Disasters and Tragic Events: An Encyclopedia of Catastrophes in American History, 581–585*. Santa Barbara, CA: ABC-CLIO, 2014.

USA Patriot Act, 115 Stat. 272, 2001.

Documents

DOCUMENT 1

"The Wounded Who Do Not Fight"

Kate Richards O'Hare

National Rip-Saw, XI (October 1914): 6–7.

With bated breath the world is beginning to talk of the cost of the European orgy of blood and murder. Bankers figure the amount in dollars and cents, capitalists estimate the wasted labor and merchants reckon the ruined commodities. A few tender hearted are even counting the frightful waste of human life and attempting to reckon the toll of suffering and anguish.

The wise men disagree as wise men are wont to do, on details. The money changers wrangle as to whether the cost in the good coin of the realm is forty million or fifty-four million dollars per day, the capitalists argue over a few billions more or less of wasted labor and the merchants differ several billions as to the value of wasted commodities; but no statistics so far have been produced setting forth the cost of the European war to those who in the last analysis must bear the brunt and pay the toll—THE WOMANHOOD OF THE RACE.

A million men march out to the call of the bugle and three million women are left behind to mourn; for back of each soldier there is mother and sister, wife or sweetheart. The mother-heart stifles with the agony of dread for the son who has marched away; the wife-soul cowers in stunned misery for the father of her children, torn from her side and the maiden longs for the lover who never will be father to the children who never can be born.

Two mighty armies clash, in the roar of cannons and the rattle of musketry two groups of men hurl the messengers of death into each others ranks, and when the last cannon has belched forth its message of death and the last Mauser has sung its spiteful song of hate, one side declares it victory, the other admits defeat. Then each side goes out to count its loss and bury its dead. Forty thousand fighting men are lost, costly implements of warfare are mere twisted bits of scrap steel, cities are razed, fields laid waste; homes are in ashes and the vineyards are red with the vintage from human veins. Out from the piled up masses of rotting carcasses comes the feeble babble of the wounded not yet dead.

Ruin and death and chaos prevail.

We can count the dead men and write their number in round figures; we can count the cost of making new implements of war and reckon the money value of the crops laid waste, of the cities razed and of the homes in ashes. We may even speculate on the human agony represented by the dead men with faces cold and stark upturned to the sky or purpling under the autumn sun; we may shudder at the cry of dying men babbling in the delirium of gaping wounds and burning thirst—but who can or ever will dream of measuring the agony of the wounded who never fought—THE WOMEN WHO STAYED AT HOME!

For the men who march away there is the urge of the blood lust unleashed by the lure of cunning lies used to appeal to man's lowest passions. For the men who answer to the bugle call there is the impetus of crashing martial music and the hypnotism of being carried by the human flood. For the men who fall in the crash of battle there is the surge of elemental passions and the swift oblivion of death borne on a singing bullet. To the wounded entangled in the piles of festering dead, kind nature brings the forgetfulness of delirium and many a wounded soldier with his head pillowed on the torn body of his dead comrade, babbles of limpid brooks, ripening vineyards and a maiden's kisses. BUT WHAT OF THE WOMEN LEFT AT HOME?

For the WOMEN, THE WOUNDED WHO DO NOT FIGHT, THE DEATH STRICKEN WHO MAY NOT DIE, there is all of the seething hell of war and none of its lure and passion. For the womanhood of the race no martial music crashes; the human flood swells, ebbs and leaves them stranded in the quagmires of despair; no singing bullet or roaring cannon brings the deep oblivion of death and no merciful delirium brings the sweet dreams of happier days. For the helpless victims of war's cursed madness there is only the agony of the damned, the unrelieved misery of suspense, hopelessness and dumb despair.

All over Europe from the anguished hearts of mothers arises the wail of Naomi, "I am old and barren and there is no more fruit in my womb." Wives crouch in the shattered ruins of once happy homes or drag whimpering children out of the reek and stench of war and face the dreary problem of brooding fatherless fledglings amidst the bitter curse of poverty. Maidens fall prey to the rapine waged by men driven mad by the blood and lust of war and are despoiled of the flower of their womanhood before it ever blossoms.

It is the women of Europe who pay the price while war rages, and it will be the women who will pay again when war has run its bloody course and Europe sinks down into the slough of poverty like a harried beast too spent to wage the fight. It will be the sonless mothers who will bend their shoulders to the plow and wield in age-palsied hands the reaphook.

It will be the husbandless women who will level the graves and replant the grapevines in the blood fertilized lands of Europe. It will be tiny hands of fatherless children who will wield the hoe and man the machines in the factories. It will be the maidens who will never know wife- or motherhood who will bear the burdens that should have lain upon the shoulders of the lovers sleeping in the unmarked graves of an alien land. Upon the shoulders of women and children will fall the grinding, blighting, blasting struggle of covering the scars of war while paying the debts piled mountain high by war.

AND THE PITY, THE TRAGEDY OF IT ALL IS THAT THE WOMEN WHO PAY THE TOLL OF AGONY, SUSPENSE AND BEREAVEMENT WHILE WAR RAGES AND WHO PAY THE PRICE IN POVERTY AND TOIL WHEN WAR HAS SPENT ITS FURY, HAVE NO VOICE IN THE PARLIAMENTS OF THE WORLD AND NO POWER TO DECLARE THAT WAR SHALL OR SHALL NOT RAGE.

Source: Kate Richards O'Hare, "The Wounded Who Do Not Fight," *National Rip-Saw*, XI (October 1914): 6–7. (womhist.alexanderstreet.com/kro/doc002.htm. Accessed March 4, 2016).

DOCUMENT 2

President Woodrow Wilson Asks Congress to Declare War in Order for "The World Must Be Safe for Democracy"

President Woodrow Wilson

April 2, 1917

I have called the Congress into extraordinary session because there are serious, very serious, choices of policy to be made, and made immediately, which it was neither right nor constitutionally permissible that I should assume the responsibility of making. On the 3rd of February last, I officially laid before you the extraordinary announcement of the Imperial German government that on and after the 1st day of February it was its purpose to put aside all restraints of law or of humanity and use its submarines to sink every vessel that sought to approach either the ports of Great Britain and Ireland or the western coasts of Europe or any of the ports controlled by the enemies of Germany within the Mediterranean.

That had seemed to be the object of the German submarine warfare earlier in the war, but since April of last year the Imperial government had somewhat restrained the commanders of its undersea craft in conformity with its promise then given to us that passenger boats should not be sunk and that due warning would be given to all other vessels which its submarines might seek to destroy, when no resistance was offered or escape attempted, and care taken that their crews were given at least a fair chance to save their lives in their open boats. The precautions taken were meager and haphazard enough, as was proved in distressing instance after instance in the progress of the cruel and unmanly business, but a certain degree of restraint was observed.

The new policy has swept every restriction aside. Vessels of every kind, whatever their flag, their character, their cargo, their destination, their errand, have been ruthlessly sent to the bottom without warning and without thought of help or mercy for those on board, the vessels of friendly neutrals along with those of belligerents. Even hospital ships and ships carrying relief to the sorely bereaved and stricken people of Belgium, though the latter were provided with safe conduct through the proscribed areas by the German government itself and were distinguished by unmistakable marks of identity, have been sunk with the same reckless lack of compassion or of principle.

I was for a little while unable to believe that such things would in fact be done by any government that had hitherto subscribed to the humane practices of civilized nations. International law had its origin in the attempt to set up some law which would be respected and observed upon the seas, where no nation had right of dominion and where lay the free highways of the world. By painful stage after stage has that law been built up, with meager enough results, indeed, after all was accomplished that could be accomplished, but always with a clear view, at least, of what the heart and conscience of mankind demanded.

This minimum of right the German government has swept aside under the plea of retaliation and necessity and because it had no weapons which it could use at sea except these which it is impossible to employ as it is employing them without throwing to the winds all scruples of humanity or of respect for the understandings that were supposed to underlie the intercourse of the world. I am not now thinking of the loss of property involved, immense and serious as that is, but only of the wanton and wholesale destruction of the lives of noncombatants, men, women, and children, engaged in pursuits which have always, even in the darkest periods of modern history, been deemed innocent and legitimate. Property can be paid for; the lives of peaceful and innocent people cannot be.

The present German submarine warfare against commerce is a warfare against mankind. It is a war against all nations. American ships have been sunk, American lives taken in ways which it has stirred us very deeply to learn of; but the ships and people of other neutral and friendly nations have been sunk and overwhelmed in the waters in the same way. There has been no discrimination. The challenge is to all mankind.

Each nation must decide for itself how it will meet it. The choice we make for ourselves must be made with a moderation of counsel and a temperateness of judgment befitting our character and our motives as a nation. We must put excited feeling away. Our motive will not be revenge or the victorious assertion of the physical might of the nation, but only the vindication of right, of human right, of which we are only a single champion.

When I addressed the Congress on the 26th of February last, I thought that it would suffice to assert our neutral rights with arms, our right to use the seas against unlawful interference, our right to keep our people safe against unlawful violence. But armed neutrality, it now appears, is impracticable. Because submarines are in effect outlaws when used as the German submarines have been used against merchant shipping, it is impossible to defend ships against their attacks as the law of nations has assumed that merchantmen would defend themselves against privateers or cruisers, visible craft giving chase upon the open sea.

It is common prudence in such circumstances, grim necessity indeed, to endeavor to destroy them before they have shown their own intention. They must be dealt with upon sight, if dealt with at all. The German government denies the right of neutrals to use arms at all within the areas of the sea which it has proscribed, even in the defense of rights which no modern publicist has ever before questioned their right to defend. The intimation is conveyed that the armed guards which we have placed on our merchant ships will be treated as beyond the pale of law and subject to be dealt with as pirates would be.

Armed neutrality is ineffectual enough at best; in such circumstances and in the face of such pretensions it is worse than ineffectual: it is likely only to produce what it was meant to prevent; it is practically certain to draw us into the war without either the rights or the effectiveness of belligerents. There is one choice we cannot make, we are incapable of making: we will not choose the path of submission and suffer the most sacred rights of our nation and our people to be ignored or violated. The wrongs against which we now array ourselves are no common wrongs; they cut to the very roots of human life.

With a profound sense of the solemn and even tragical character of the step I am taking and of the grave responsibilities which it involves, but in unhesitating obedience to what I deem my constitutional duty, I advise that the Congress declare the recent course of the Imperial German government to be in fact nothing less than war against the government and people of the United States; that it formally accept the status of belligerent which has thus been thrust upon it; and that it take immediate steps, not only to put the country in a more thorough state of defense but also to exert all its power and employ all its resources to bring the government of the German Empire to terms and end the war.

What this will involve is clear. It will involve the utmost practicable cooperation in counsel and action with the governments now at war with

Germany and, as incident to that. The extension to those governments of the most liberal financial credits, in order that our resources may so far as possible be added to theirs. It will involve the organization and mobilization of all the material resources of the country to supply the materials of war and serve the incidental needs of the nation in the most abundant and yet the most economical and efficient way possible. It will involve the immediate full equipment of the Navy in all respects but particularly in supplying it with the best means of dealing with the enemy's submarines. It will involve the immediate addition to the armed forces of the United States already provided for by law in case of war at least 500,000 men, who should, in my opinion, be chosen upon the principle of universal liability to service, and also the authorization of subsequent additional increments of equal force so soon as they may be needed and can be handled in training.

It will involve also, of course, the granting of adequate credits to the government, sustained, I hope, so far as they can equitably be sustained by the present generation, by well-conceived taxation. I say sustained so far as may be equitable by taxation because it seems to me that it would be most unwise to base the credits which will now be necessary entirely on money borrowed. It is our duty, I most respectfully urge, to protect our people so far as we may against the very serious hardships and evils which would be likely to arise out of the inflation which would be produced by vast loans.

In carrying out the measures by which these things are to be accomplished, we should keep constantly in mind the wisdom of interfering as little as possible in our own preparation and in the equipment of our own military forces with the duty—for it will be a very practical duty—of supplying the nations already at war with Germany with the materials which they can obtain only from us or by our assistance. They are in the field and we should help them in every way to be effective there.

I shall take the liberty of suggesting, through the several executive departments of the government, for the consideration of your committees, measures for the accomplishment of the several objects I have mentioned. I hope that it will be your pleasure to deal with them as having been framed after very careful thought by the branch of the government upon which the responsibility of conducting the war and safeguarding the nation will most directly fall.

While we do these things, these deeply momentous things, let us be very clear, and make very clear to all the world, what our motives and our objects are. My own thought has not been driven from its habitual and normal course by the unhappy events of the last two months, and I do not believe that the thought of the nation has been altered or clouded by them. I have exactly the same things in mind now that I had in mind when I addressed the

Senate on the 22nd of January last; the same that I had in mind when I addressed the Congress on the 3rd of February and on the 26th of February.

Our object now, as then, is to vindicate the principles of peace and justice in the life of the world as against selfish and autocratic power and to set up among the really free and self-governed peoples of the world such a concert of purpose and of action as will henceforth ensure the observance of those principles. Neutrality is no longer feasible or desirable where the peace of the world is involved and the freedom of its peoples, and the menace to that peace and freedom lies in the existence of autocratic governments backed by organized force which is controlled wholly by their will, not by the will of their people. We have seen the last of neutrality in such circumstances. We are at the beginning of an age in which it will be insisted that the same standards of conduct and of responsibility for wrong done shall be observed among nations and their governments that are observed among the individual citizens of civilized states.

We have no quarrel with the German people. We have no feeling toward them but one of sympathy and friendship. It was not upon their impulse that their government acted in entering this war. It was not with their previous knowledge or approval. It was a war determined upon as wars used to be determined upon in the old, unhappy days when peoples were nowhere consulted by their rulers and wars were provoked and waged in the interest of dynasties or of little groups of ambitious men who were accustomed to use their fellowmen as pawns and tools.

Self-governed nations do not fill their neighbor states with spies or set the course of intrigue to bring about some critical posture of affairs which will give them an opportunity to strike and make conquest. Such designs can be successfully worked out only under cover and where no one has the right to ask questions. Cunningly contrived plans of deception or aggression, carried, it may be, from generation to generation, can be worked out and kept from the light only within the privacy of courts or behind the carefully guarded confidences of a narrow and privileged class. They are happily impossible where public opinion commands and insists upon full information concerning all the nation's affairs.

A steadfast concert for peace can never be maintained except by a partnership of democratic nations. No autocratic government could be trusted to keep faith within it or observe its covenants. It must be a league of honor, a partnership of opinion. Intrigue would eat its vitals away; the plottings of inner circles who could plan what they would and render account to no one would be a corruption seated at its very heart. Only free peoples can hold their purpose and their honor steady to a common end and prefer the interests of mankind to any narrow interest of their own.

Does not every American feel that assurance has been added to our hope for the future peace of the world by the wonderful and heartening things that have been happening within the last few weeks in Russia? Russia was known by those who knew it best to have been always in fact democratic at heart, in all the vital habits of her thought, in all the intimate relationships of her people that spoke their natural instinct, their habitual attitude toward life. The autocracy that crowned the summit of her political structure, long as it had stood and terrible as was the reality of its power, was not in fact Russian in origin, character, or purpose; and now it has been shaken off and the great, generous Russian people have been added in all their naive majesty and might to the forces that are fighting for freedom in the world, for justice, and for peace. Here is a fit partner for a League of Honor.

One of the things that has served to convince us that the Prussian autocracy was not and could never be our friend is that from the very outset of the present war it has filled our unsuspecting communities and even our offices of government with spies and set criminal intrigues everywhere afoot against our national unity of counsel, our peace within and without, our industries and our commerce. Indeed, it is now evident that its spies were here even before the war began; and it is unhappily not a matter of con-jecture but a fact proved in our courts of justice that the intrigues which have more than once come perilously near to disturbing the peace and dislocating the industries of the country have been carried on at the instigation, with the support, and even under the personal direction of official agents of the Imperial government accredited to the government of the United States.

Even in checking these things and trying to extirpate them, we have sought to put the most generous interpretation possible upon them because we knew that their source lay, not in any hostile feeling or purpose of the German people toward us (who were no doubt as ignorant of them as we ourselves were) but only in the selfish designs of a government that did what it pleased and told its people nothing. But they have played their part in serving to convince us at last that that government entertains no real friend-ship for us and means to act against our peace and security at its convenience. That it means to stir up enemies against us at our very doors the intercepted note to the German minister at Mexico City is eloquent evidence.

We are accepting this challenge of hostile purpose because we know that in such a government, following such methods, we can never have a friend; and that in the presence of its organized power, always lying in wait to accomplish we know not what purpose, there can be no assured security for the democratic governments of the world. We are now about to accept [the] gage [the challenge] of battle with this natural foe to liberty and shall, if necessary, spend the whole force of the nation to check and nullify its pretensions and its power. We are glad, now that we see the facts with no veil of false pretense about them, to fight thus for the ultimate peace of the world and for the liberation of its peoples, the German peoples included: for the rights of nations great and small and the privilege of men everywhere to choose their way of life and of obedience.

The world must be made safe for democracy. Its peace must be planted upon the tested foundations of political liberty. We have no selfish ends to serve. We desire no conquest, no dominion. We seek no indemnities for ourselves, no material compensation for the sacrifices we shall freely make. We are but one of the champions of the rights of mankind. We shall be satisfied when those rights have been made as secure as the faith and the freedom of nations can make them.

Just because we fight without rancor and without selfish object, seeking nothing for ourselves but what we shall wish to share with all free peoples, we shall, I feel confident, conduct our operations as belligerents without passion and ourselves observe with proud punctilio the principles of right and of fair play we profess to be fighting for.

I have said nothing of the governments allied with the Imperial government of Germany because they have not made war upon us or challenged us to defend our right and our honor. The Austro-Hungarian government has, indeed, avowed its unqualified endorsement and acceptance of the reckless and lawless submarine warfare adopted now without disguise by the Imperial German government, and it has therefore not been possible for this government to receive Count Tarnowski, the ambassador recently accredited to this government by the Imperial and Royal government of Austria-Hungary; but that government has not actually engaged in warfare against citizens of the United States on the seas, and I take the liberty, for the present at least, of postponing a discussion of our relations with the authorities at Vienna. We enter this war only where we are clearly forced into it because there are no other means of defending our rights.

It will be all the easier for us to conduct ourselves as belligerents in a high spirit of right and fairness because we act without animus, not in enmity toward a people or with the desire to bring any injury or disadvantage upon them, but only in armed opposition to an irresponsible government which has thrown aside all considerations of humanity and of right and is running amuck. We are, let me say again, the sincere friends of the German people, and shall desire nothing so much as the early reestablishment of intimate relations of mutual advantage between us—however hard it may be for them, for the time being, to believe that this is spoken from our hearts.

We have borne with their present government through all these bitter months because of that friendship—exercising a patience and forbearance which would otherwise have been impossible. We shall, happily, still have an opportunity to prove that friendship in our daily attitude and actions toward the millions of men and women of German birth and native sympathy who live among us and share our life, and we shall be proud to prove it toward all who are in fact loyal to their neighbors and to the government in the hour of test. They are, most of them, as true and loyal Americans as if they had never known any other fealty or allegiance. They will be prompt to stand with us in rebuking and restraining the few who may be of a different mind and purpose. If there should be disloyalty, it will be dealt with with a firm hand of stern repression; but, if it lifts its head at all, it will lift it only here and there and without countenance except from a lawless and malignant few.

It is a distressing and oppressive duty, gentlemen of the Congress, which I have performed in thus addressing you. There are, it may be, many months of fiery trial and sacrifice ahead of us. It is a fearful thing to lead this great peaceful people into war, into the most terrible and disastrous of all wars, civilization itself seeming to be in the balance. But the right is more precious than peace, and we shall fight for the things which we have always carried nearest our hearts—for democracy, for the right of those who submit to authority to have a voice in their own governments, for the rights and liberties of small nations, for a universal dominion of right by such a concert of free peoples as shall bring peace and safety to all nations and make the world itself at last free.

To such a task we can dedicate our lives and our fortunes, everything that we are and everything that we have, with the pride of those who know that the day has come when America is privileged to spend her blood and her might for the principles that gave her birth and happiness and the peace which she has treasured. God helping her, she can do no other.

Source: President Woodrow Wilson Asks Congress to Declare War in Order for "The World Must Be Safe for Democracy." (April 2, 1917). (http://www.ourdocuments.gov/doc.php?doc=61&page=transcript. Accessed February 7, 2016).

Emma Goldman

Address to the Jury During Her Trial in Violation of the Espionage Act

Emma Goldman

July 9, 1917

Gentlemen of the Jury:

As in the case of my co-defendant, Alexander Berkman, this is also the first time in my life I have ever addressed a jury. I once had occasion to speak to three judges.

On the day after our arrest it was given out by the U.S. Marshal and the District Attorney's office that the "big fish" of the No-Conscription activities had been caught, and that there would be no more trouble-makers and disturbers to interfere with the highly democratic effort of the Government to conscript its young manhood for the European slaughter. What a pity that the faithful servants of the Government, personified in the U.S. Marshal and the District Attorney, should have used such a weak and flimsy net for their big catch. The moment the anglers pulled their heavily laden net ashore, it broke, and all the labor was so much wasted energy.

The methods employed by Marshal McCarthy and his hosts of heroic warriors were sensational enough to satisfy the famous circus men, Barnum & Bailey. A dozen or more heroes dashing up two flights of stairs, prepared to stake their lives for their country, only to discover the two dangerous disturbers and trouble-makers, Alexander Berkman and Emma Goldman, in their separate offices, quietly at work at their desks, wielding not a sword, nor a gun or a bomb, but merely their pens! Verily, it required courage to catch such big fish.

To be sure, two officers equipped with a warrant would have sufficed to carry out the business of arresting the defendants Alexander Berkman and Emma Goldman. Even the police know that neither of them is in the habit of running away or hiding under the bed. But the farce-comedy had to be properly staged if the Marshal and the District Attorney were to earn immortality. Hence the sensational arrest; hence also, the raid upon the offices of The Blast, Mother Earth, and the No-Conscription League.

In their zeal to save the country from the trouble-makers, the Marshal and his helpers did not even consider it necessary to produce a search warrant. After all, what matters a mere scrap of paper when one is called upon to raid the offices of Anarchists! Of what consequence is the sanctity of property, the right of privacy, to officials in their dealings with Anarchists! In our day of military training for battle, an Anarchist office is an appropriate camping ground. Would the gentlemen who came with Marshal McCarthy have dared to go into the offices of Morgan, or Rockefeller, or of any of those men without a search warrant? They never showed us the search warrant, although we asked them for it. Nevertheless, they turned our office into a battlefield, so that when they were through with it, it looked like invaded Belgium, with the only difference that the invaders were not Prussian barbarians but good American patriots bent on making New York safe for democracy.

The stage having been appropriately set for the three-act comedy, and the first act successfully played by carrying off the villains in a madly dashing automobile—which broke every traffic regulation and barely escaped crushing every one in its way—the second act proved even more ludicrous. Fifty thousand dollars bail was demanded, and real estate refused when offered by a man whose property is rated at three hundred thousand dollars, and that after the District Attorney had considered and, in fact, promised to accept the property for one of the defendants, Alexander Berkman, thus breaking every right guaranteed even to the most heinous criminal.

Finally the third act, played by the Government in this court during the last week. The pity of it is that the prosecution knows so little of dramatic construction, else it would have equipped itself with better dramatic material to sustain the continuity of the play. As it was, the third act fell flat, utterly, and presents the question, Why such a tempest in a teapot? Gentlemen of the jury, my comrade and co-defendant having carefully and thoroughly gone into the evidence presented by the prosecution, and having demonstrated its entire failure to prove the charge of conspiracy or any overt acts to carry out that conspiracy, I shall not impose upon your patience by going over the same ground, except to emphasize a few points. To charge people with having conspired to do something which they have been engaged in doing most of their lives, namely their campaign against war, militarism and conscription as contrary to the best interests of humanity, is an insult to human intelligence.

And how was that charge proven? By the fact that Mother Earth and The Blast were printed by the same printer and bound in the same bindery. By the further evidence that the same expressman had delivered the two publications! And by the still more illuminating fact that on June 2nd Mother Earth and The Blast were given to a reporter at his request, if you please, and gratis.

Gentlemen of the jury, you saw the reporter who testified to this overt act. Did anyone of you receive the impression that the man was of con-scriptable age, and if not, in what possible way is the giving of Mother Earth to a reporter for news purposes proof demonstrating the overt act?

It was brought out by our witnesses that the Mother Earth magazine has been published for twelve years; that it was never held up, and that it has always gone through the U.S. mail as second-class mail matter. It was further proven that the magazine appeared each month about the first or second, and that it was sold or given away at the office to whoever wanted a copy. Where, then, is the overt act?

Just as the prosecution has utterly failed to prove the charge of con-spiracy, so has it also failed to prove the overt act by the flimsy testimony that Mother Earth was given to a reporter. The same holds good regarding The Blast.

Gentlemen of the jury, the District Attorney must have learned from the reporters the gist of the numerous interviews which they had with us. Why did he not examine them as to whether or not we had counseled young men not to register? That would have been a more direct way of getting at the facts. In the case of the reporter from the New York Times, there can be no doubt that the man would have been only too happy to accommodate the District Attorney with the required information. A man who disregards every principle of decency and ethics of his profession as a newspaper man, by turning material given him as news over to the District Attorney, would have been glad to oblige a friend. Why did Mr. Content neglect such a golden opportunity? Was it not because the reporter of the Times, like all the other reporters, must have told the District Attorney that the two defendants stated, on each and every occasion, they would not tell people not to register?

Perhaps the Times reporter refused to go to the extent of perjuring himself. Patrolmen and detectives are not so timid in such matters. Hence Mr. Randolph and Mr. Cadell, to rescue the situation. Imagine employing tenth-rate stenographers to report the very important speeches of dangerous trouble-makers!

What lack of forethought and efficiency on the part of the District Attorney! But even these two members of the police department failed to prove by their notes that we advised people not to register. But since they had to produce something incriminating against Anarchists, they conveniently resorted to the old standby, always credited to us, "We believe in violence and we will use violence."

Assuming, gentlemen of the jury, that this sentence was really used at the meeting of May 18th, it would still fail to prove the indictment which charges conspiracy and overt acts to carry out the conspiracy. And that is all we are charged with. Not violence, not Anarchism. I will go further and say, that had the indictment been for the advocacy of violence, you gentlemen of the jury, would still have to render a verdict of "Not Guilty," since the mere belief in a thing or even the announcement that you would carry out that belief, cannot possibly constitute a crime.

However, I wish to say emphatically that no such expression as "We believe in violence and we will use violence" was uttered at the meeting of May 18th, or at any other meeting. I could not have employed such a phrase, as there was no occasion for it. If for no other reason, it is because I want my lectures and speeches to be coherent and logical. The sentence credited to me is neither.

I have read to you my position toward political violence from a lengthy essay called "The Psychology of Political Violence."

But to make that position clearer and simpler, I wish to say that I am a social student. It is my mission in life to ascertain the cause of our social evils and of our social difficulties. As a student of social wrongs it is my aim to diagnose a wrong. To simply condemn the man who has committed an act of political violence, in order to save my skin, would be as unpardonable as it would be on the part of the physician, who is called to diagnose a case, to condemn the patient because the patient has tuberculosis, cancer, or some other disease. The honest, earnest, sincere physician does not only prescribe medicine, he tries to find out the cause of the disease. And if the patient is at all capable as to means, the doctor will say to him, "Get out of this putrid air, get out of the factory, get out of the place where your lungs are being infected." He will not merely give him medicine. He will tell him the cause of the disease. And that is precisely my position in regard to acts of violence. That is what I have said on every platform. I have attempted to explain the cause and the reason for acts of political violence.

It is organized violence on top which creates individual violence at the bottom. It is the accumulated indignation against organized wrong, organized crime, organized injustice which drives the political offender to his act. To condemn him means to be blind to the causes which make him. I can no more do it, nor have I the right to, than the physician who were to condemn the patient for his disease. You and I and all of us who remain indifferent to the crimes of poverty, of war, of human degradation, are equally responsible for the act committed by the political offender. May I therefore be permitted to say, in the words of a great teacher: "He who is without sin among you, let him cast the first stone." Does that mean advocating violence? You might as well accuse Jesus of advocating prostitution, because He took the part of the prostitute, Mary Magdalene.

Gentlemen of the jury, the meeting of the 18th of May was called primarily for the purpose of voicing the position of the conscientious objector and to point out the evils of conscription. Now, who and what is the conscientious objector? Is he really a shirker, a slacker, or a coward? To call him that is to be guilty of dense ignorance of the forces which impel men and women to stand out against the whole world like a glittering lone star upon a dark horizon. The conscientious objector is impelled by what President Wilson in his speech of Feb. 3, 1917, called "the righteous passion for justice upon which all war, all structure of family, State and of mankind must rest as the ultimate base of our existence and our liberty." The righteous passion for justice which can never express itself in human slaughter— that is the force which makes the conscientious objector. Poor indeed is the country which fails to recognize the importance of that new type of humanity as the "ultimate base of our existence and liberty." It will find itself barren of that which makes for character and quality in its people.

The meeting of May 18th was held before the Draft Bill had actually gone into effect. The President signed it late in the evening of the 18th. Whatever was said at that meeting, even if I had counseled young men not to register, that meeting cannot serve as proof of an overt act. Why, then, has the Prosecuting Attorney dwelt so much, at such length, and with such pains on that meeting, and so little on the other meetings held on the eve of registration and after? Is it not because the District Attorney knew that we had no stenographic notes of that meeting? He knew it because he was approached by Mr. Weinberger and other friends for a copy of the transcript, which request he refused. Evidently, the District Attorney felt safe to use the notes of a patrolman and a detective, knowing that they would swear to anything their superiors wanted. I never like to accuse anyone—I wouldn't go so far as my co-defendant, Mr. Berkman, in saying that the District Attorney doctored the document; I don't know whether he did or not. But I do know that Patrolman Randolph and Detective Cadell doctored the notes, for the simple reason that I didn't say those things. But though we could not produce our own stenographic notes, we have been able to prove by men and women of unimpeachable character and high intelligence that the notes of Randolph are utterly false. We have also proven beyond a reasonable doubt, and Mr. Content did not dare question our proof, that at the Hunts' Point Palace, held on the eve of registration, I expressly stated that I cannot and will not tell people not to register. We have further proven that this was my definite stand, which was explained in my statement sent from Springfield and read at the meeting of May 23rd.

When we go through the entire testimony given on behalf of the prosecution, I insist that there is not one single point to sustain the indictment for conspiracy or to prove the overt acts we are supposed to have committed. But we were even compelled to bring a man eighty years of age to the witness stand in order to stop, if possible, any intention to drag in the question of German money. It is true, and I appreciate it, that Mr. Content said he had no knowledge of it. But, gentlemen of the jury, somebody from the District Attorney's office or someone from the Marshal's office must have given out the statement that a bank receipt for $2,400 was found in my office and must have told the newspapers the fake story of German money. As if we would ever touch German money, or Russian money, or American money coming from the ruling class, to advance our ideas! But in order to forestall any suspicion, any insinuation, in order to stand clear before you, we were compelled to bring an old man here to inform you that he has been a radical all his life, that he is interested in our ideas, and that he is the man who contributed the money for radical purposes and for the work of Miss Goldman.

Gentlemen of the jury, you will be told by the Court, I am sure, that when you render a verdict you must be convinced beyond a reasonable doubt; that you must not assume that we are guilty before we are proven guilty; and that it is your duty to assume that we are innocent. And yet, as a matter of fact, the burden of proof has been laid upon us. We had to bring witnesses. If we had had time we could have brought fifty more witnesses, each corroborating the others. Some of those people have no relation with us. Some are writers, poets, contributors to the most conventional magazines. Is it likely that they would swear to something in our favor if it were not the truth? Therefore I insist, as did my co-defendant Alexander Berkman, that the prosecution has made a very poor showing in proving the conspiracy or any overt act.

Gentlemen of the jury, we have been in public life for twenty-seven years. We have been hauled into court, in and out of season—we have never denied our position. Even the police know that Emma Goldman and Alexander Berkman are not shirkers. You have had occasion during this trial to convince yourselves that we do not deny. We have gladly and proudly claimed responsibility, not only for what we ourselves have said and written, but even for things written by others and with which we did not agree. Is it plausible, then, that we would go through the ordeal, trouble and expense of a lengthy trial to escape responsibility in this instance? A thousand times no! But we refuse to be tried on a trumped-up charge, or to be convicted by perjured testimony, merely because we are Anarchists and hated by the class whom we have openly fought for many years.

Gentlemen, during our examination of talesmen, when we asked whether you would be prejudiced against us if it were proven that we propagated ideas and opinions contrary to those held by the majority, you were instructed by the Court to say, "If they are within the law." But what the Court did not tell you is, that no new faith—not even the most humane and peaceable—has ever been considered "within the law" by those who were in power. The history of human growth is at the same time the history of every new idea heralding the approach of a brighter dawn, and the brighter dawn has always been considered illegal, outside of the law.

Gentlemen of the jury, most of you, I take it, are believers in the teachings of Jesus. Bear in mind that he was put to death by those who considered his views as being against the law. I also take it that you are proud of your Americanism. Remember that those who fought and bled for your liberties were in their time considered as being against the law, as dangerous disturbers and trouble-makers. They not only preached violence, but they carried out their ideas by throwing tea into the Boston harbor. They said that "Resistance to tyranny is obedience to God." They wrote a dangerous document called the Declaration of Independence. A document which continues to be dangerous to this day, and for the circulation of which a young man was sentenced to ninety days prison in a New York Court, only the other day. They were the Anarchists of their time—they were never within the law.

Your Government is allied with the French Republic. Need I call your attention to the historic fact that the great upheaval in France was brought about by extra-legal means? The Dant[on]s, the Robespierres, the Marats, the Herberts, aye even the man who is responsible for the most stirring revolutionary music, the Marseillaise (which unfortunately has deteriorated into a war tune) even Camille Desmoulins, were never within the law. But for those great pioneers and rebels, France would have continued under the yoke of the idle Louis XVI, to whom the sport of shooting jack rabbits was more important than the destiny of the people of France.

Ah, gentlemen, on the very day when we were being tried for conspiracy and overt acts, your city officials and representatives welcomed with music and festivities the Russian Commission. Are you aware of the fact that nearly all of the members of that Commission have only recently been released from exile? The ideas they propagated were never within the law. For nearly a hundred years, from 1825 to 1917, the Tree of Liberty in Russia was watered by the blood of her martyrs. No greater heroism, no nobler lives had ever been dedicated to humanity. Not one of them worked within the law.

I could continue to enumerate almost endlessly the hosts of men and women in every land and in every period whose ideas and ideals redeemed the world because they were not within the law. Never can a new idea move within the law. It matters not whether that idea pertains to political and social changes or to any other domain of human thought and expression—to science, literature, music; in fact, everything that makes for freedom and joy and beauty must refuse to move within the law. How can it be otherwise? The law is stationary, fixed, mechanical, "a chariot wheel" which grinds all alike without regard to time, place and condition, without ever taking into account cause and effect, without ever going into the complexity of the human soul.

Progress knows nothing of fixity. It cannot be pressed into a definite mould. It cannot bow to the dictum, "I have ruled," "I am the regulating finger of God." Progress is ever renewing, ever becoming, ever changing—*never is it within the law.*

If that be crime, we are criminals even like Jesus, Socrates, Galileo, Bruno, John Brown and scores of others. We are in good company, among those whom Havelock Ellis, the greatest living psychologist, describes as the political criminals recognized by the whole civilized world, except America, as men and women who out of deep love for humanity, out of a passionate reverence for liberty and an all-absorbing devotion to an ideal are ready to pay for their faith even with their blood. We cannot do otherwise if we are to be true to ourselves—we know that the political criminal is the precursor of human progress—the political criminal of today must needs be the hero, the martyr and the saint of the new age.

But, says the Prosecuting Attorney, the press and the unthinking rabble, in high and low station, "that is a dangerous doctrine and unpatriotic at this time." No doubt it is. But are we to be held responsible for something which is as unchangeable and unalienable as the very stars hanging in the heavens unto time and all eternity?

Gentlemen of the jury, we respect your patriotism. We would not, if we could, have you change its meaning for yourself. But may there not be different kinds of patriotism as there are different kinds of liberty? I for one cannot believe that love of one's country must needs consist in blindness to its social faults, to deafness to its social discords, of inarticulation to its social wrongs. Neither can I believe that the mere accident of birth in a certain country or the mere scrap of a citizen's paper constitutes the love of country.

I know many people—I am one of them—who were not born here, nor have they applied for citizenship, and who yet love America with deeper passion and greater intensity than many natives whose patriotism manifests itself by pulling, kicking, and insulting those who do not rise when the national anthem is played. Our patriotism is that of the man who loves a woman with open eyes. He is enchanted by her beauty, yet he sees her faults. So we, too, who know America, love her beauty, her richness, her great possibilities; we love her mountains, her canyons, her forests, her Niagara, and her deserts—above all do we love the people that have produced her wealth, her artists who have created beauty, her great apostles who dream and work for liberty—but with the same passionate emotion we hate her superficiality, her cant, her corruption, her mad, unscrupulous worship at the altar of the Golden Calf.

We say that if America has entered the war to make the world safe for democracy, she must first make democracy safe in America. How else is the world to take America seriously, when democracy at home is daily being outraged, free speech suppressed, peaceable assemblies broken up by over-bearing and brutal gangsters in uniform; when free press is curtailed and every independent opinion gagged. Verily, poor as we are in democracy, how can we give of it to the world? We further say that a democracy conceived in the military servitude of the masses, in their economic enslave-ment, and nurtured in their tears and blood, is not democracy at all. It is despotism—the cumulative result of a chain of abuses which, according to that dangerous document, the Declaration of Independence, the people have the right to overthrow.

The District Attorney has dragged in our Manifesto, and he has empha-sized the passage, "Resist conscription." Gentlemen of the jury, please remember that that is not the charge against us. But admitting that the Manifesto contains the expression, "Resist conscription," may I ask you, is there only one kind of resistance? Is there only the resistance which means the gun, the bayonet, the bomb or flying machine? Is there not another kind of resistance? May not the people simply fold their hands and declare, "We will not fight when we do not believe in the necessity of war"? May not the people who believe in the repeal of the Conscription Law, because it is unconstitutional, express their opposition in word and by pen, in meetings and in other ways? What right has the District Attorney to interpret that particular passage to suit himself? Moreover, gentlemen of the jury, I insist that the indictment against us does not refer to conscription. We are charged with a conspiracy against registration. And in no way or manner has the prosecution proven that we are guilty of conspiracy or that we have com-mitted an overt act.

Gentlemen of the jury, you are not called upon to accept our views, to approve of them or to justify them. You are not even called upon to decide whether our views are within or against the law. You are called upon to decide whether the prosecution has proven that the defendants Emma

Goldman and Alexander Berkman have conspired to urge people not to register. And whether their speeches and writings represent overt acts.

Whatever your verdict, gentlemen, it cannot possibly affect the rising tide of discontent in this country against war which, despite all boasts, is a war for conquest and military power. Neither can it affect the ever increasing opposition to conscription which is a military and industrial yoke placed upon the necks of the American people.

Least of all will your verdict affect those to whom human life is sacred, and who will not become a party to the world slaughter. Your verdict can only add to the opinion of the world as to whether or not justice and liberty are a living force in this country or a mere shadow of the past. Your verdict may, of course, affect us temporarily, in a physical sense—it can have no effect whatever upon our spirit. For even if we were convicted and found guilty and the penalty were that we be placed against a wall and shot dead, I should nevertheless cry out with the great Luther: "Here I am and here I stand and I cannot do otherwise." And gentlemen, in conclusion let me tell you that my co-defendant, Mr. Berkman, was right when he said the eyes of America are upon you. They are upon you not because of sympathy for us or agreement with Anarchism. They are upon you because it must be decided sooner or later whether we are justified in telling people that we will give them democracy in Europe, when we have no democracy here? Shall free speech and free assemblage, shall criticism and opinion—which even the espionage bill did not include—be destroyed? Shall it be a shadow of the past, the great historic American past? Shall it be trampled underfoot by any detective, or policeman, anyone who decides upon it? Or shall free speech and free press and free assemblage continue to be the heritage of the American people? Gentlemen of the jury, whatever your verdict will be, as far as we are concerned, nothing will be changed. I have held ideas all my life. I have publicly held my ideas for twenty-seven years. Nothing on earth would ever make me change my ideas except one thing; and that is, if you will prove to me that our position is wrong, untenable, or lacking in historic fact. But never would I change my ideas because I am found guilty. I may remind you of two great Americans, undoubtedly not unknown to you, gentlemen of the jury; Ralph Waldo Emerson and Henry David Thoreau. When Thoreau was placed in prison for refusing to pay taxes, he was visited by Ralph Waldo Emerson and Emerson said: "David, what are you doing in jail?" and Thoreau replied: "Ralph, what are you doing outside, when honest people are in jail for their ideals?" Gentlemen of the jury, I do not wish to influence you. I do not wish to appeal to your passions. I do not wish to influence you by the fact that I am a woman. I have no such desires and no such designs. I take it that you are sincere enough and honest enough and brave enough to render a verdict according to your convictions, beyond the shadow of a reasonable doubt.

Please forget that we are Anarchists. Forget that it is claimed that we propagated violence. Forget that something appeared in Mother Earth when I was thousands of miles away, three years ago. The bomb exploded in the apartment of anarchist Louise Berger, half-sister of Charles Berg, at 1626 Lexington Avenue between 103rd and 104th Streets, a large tenement area populated mainly by recently arrived immigrants. Forget all that, and merely consider the evidence. Have we been engaged in a conspiracy? Has that conspiracy been proven? Have we committed overt acts? Have those overt acts been proven? We for the defense say they have not been proven. And therefore your verdict must be not guilty. But whatever your decision, the struggle must go on. We are but the atoms in the incessant human struggle towards the light that shines in the darkness—the Ideal of economic, political and spiritual liberation of mankind!

Source: Emma Goldman: Address to the Jury during her trial in violation of the Espionage Act, July 9, 1917. (http://www.americanrhetoric.com/ speeches/emmagoldmanjuryaddress.htm. Accessed December 15, 2015).

The Canton, Ohio Anti-War Speech (Excerpts)

Eugene V. Debs

June 16, 1918

C omrades, friends and fellow-workers, for this very cordial greeting, this very hearty reception, I thank you all with the fullest appreciation of your interest in and your devotion to the cause for which I am to speak to you this afternoon.

To speak for labor; to plead the cause of the men and women and children who toil; to serve the working class, has always been to me a high privilege; a duty of love.

I have just returned from a visit over yonder, where three of our most loyal comrades are paying the penalty for their devotion to the cause of the working class. They have come to realize, as many of us have, that it is extremely dangerous to exercise the constitutional right of free speech in a country fighting to make democracy safe in the world.

I realize that, in speaking to you this afternoon, there are certain limitations placed upon the right of free speech. I must be exceedingly careful, prudent, as to what I say, and even more careful and prudent as to how I say it. I may not be able to say all I think; but I am not going to say anything that I do not think. I would rather a thousand times be a free soul in jail than to be a sycophant and coward in the streets. They may put those boys in jail—and some of the rest of us in jail—but they can not put the Socialist movement in jail. Those prison bars separate their bodies from ours, but their souls are here this afternoon. They are simply paying the penalty that all men have paid in all the ages of history for standing erect, and for seeking to pave the way to better conditions for mankind.

If it had not been for the men and women who, in the past, have had the moral courage to go to jail, we would still be in the jungles.

This assemblage is exceedingly good to look upon. I wish it were possible for me to give you what you are giving me this afternoon. What I say here amounts to but little; what I see here is exceedingly important. You workers in Ohio, enlisted in the greatest cause ever organized in the interest of your class, are making history today in the face of threatening opposition of all kinds—history that is going to be read with profound interest by coming generations.

There is but one thing you have to be concerned about, and that is that you keep foursquare with the principles of the international Socialist movement. It is only when you begin to compromise that trouble begins. So far as I am concerned, it does not matter what others may say, or think, or do, as long as I am sure that I am right with myself and the cause. There are so many who seek refuge in the popular side of a great question. As a Socialist, I have long since learned how to stand alone. For the last month I have been traveling over the Hoosier State; and, let me say to you, that, in all my connection with the Socialist movement, I have never seen such meetings, such enthusiasm, such unity of purpose; never have I seen such a promising outlook as there is today, notwithstanding the statement published repeatedly that our leaders have deserted us. Well, for myself, I never had much faith in leaders. I am willing to be charged with almost anything, rather than to be charged with being a leader. I am suspicious of leaders, and especially of the intellectual variety. Give me the rank and file every day in the week. If you go to the city of Washington, and you examine the pages of the Congressional Directory, you will find that almost all of those corporation lawyers and cowardly politicians, members of Congress, and misrepresentatives of the masses—you will find that almost all of them claim, in glowing terms, that they have risen from the ranks to places of eminence and distinction. I am very glad I cannot make that claim for myself. I would be ashamed to admit that I had risen from the ranks. When I rise it will be with the ranks, and not from the ranks.

When I came away from Indiana, the comrades said: "When you cross the line and get over into the Buckeye State, tell the comrades there that we are on duty and doing duty. Give them for us, a hearty greeting, and tell them that we are going to make a record this fall that will be read around the world." . . .

They who have been reading the capitalist newspapers realize what a capacity they have for lying. We have been reading them lately. They know all about the Socialist Party—the Socialist movement, except what is true.

Only the other day they took an article that I had written—and most of you have read it—most of you members of the party, at least—and they made it appear that I had undergone a marvelous transformation. I had suddenly become changed—had in fact come to my senses; I had ceased to be a wicked Socialist, and had become a respectable Socialist a patriotic Socialist—as if I had ever been anything else . . .

Why should a Socialist be discouraged on the eve of the greatest triumph in all the history of the Socialist movement? It is true that these are anxious, trying days for us all—testing days for the women and men who are upholding the banner of labor in the struggle of the working class of all the world against the exploiters of all the world; a time in which the weak and cowardly will falter and fail and desert. They lack the fiber to endure the revolutionary test; they fall away; they disappear as if they had never been. On the other hand, they who are animated by the unconquerable spirit of the social revolution; they who have the moral courage to stand erect and assert their convictions; stand by them; fight for them; go to jail or to hell for them, if need be—they are writing their names, in this crucial hour—they are writing their names in faceless letters in the history of mankind.

Those boys over yonder—those comrades of ours—and how I love them! Aye, they are my younger brothers; their very names throb in my heart, thrill in my veins, and surge in my soul. I am proud of them; they are there for us; and we are here for them. Their lips, though temporarily mute, are more eloquent than ever before; and their voice, though silent, is heard around the world.

Are we opposed to Prussian militarism? Why, we have been fighting it since the day the Socialist movement was born; and we are going to continue to fight it, day and night, until it is wiped from the face of the earth. Between us there is no truce—no compromise . . .

They would have you believe that the Socialist Party consists in the main of disloyalists and traitors. It is true in a sense not at all to their discredit. We frankly admit that we are disloyalists and traitors to the real traitors of this nation; to the gang that on the Pacific coast are trying to hang Tom Mooney and Warren Billings in spite of their well-known innocence and the protest of practically the whole civilized world.

I know Tom Mooney intimately—as if he were my own brother. He is an absolutely honest man. He had no more to do with the crime with which he was charged and for which he was convicted than I had. And if he ought to go to the gallows, so ought I. If he is guilty every man who belongs to a labor organization or to the Socialist Party is likewise guilty . . .

The other day they sentenced Kate Richards O'Hare to the penitentiary for five years. Think of sentencing a woman to the penitentiary simply for talking. The United States, under plutocratic rule, is the only country that would send a woman to prison for five years for exercising the right of free speech. If this be treason, let them make the most of it.

Let me review a bit of history in connection with this case. I have known Kate Richards O'Hare intimately for twenty years. I am familiar with her public record. Personally I know her as if she were my own sister. All who know Mrs. O'Hare know her to be a woman of unquestioned integrity. And they also know that she is a woman of unimpeachable loyalty to the Socialist movement. When she went out into North Dakota to make her speech, followed by plain-clothes men in the service of the government intent upon effecting her arrest and securing her prosecution and conviction—when she went out there, it was with the full knowledge on her part that sooner or later these detectives would accomplish their purpose. She made her speech, and that speech was deliberately misrepresented for the purpose of securing her conviction. The only testimony against her was that of a hired witness. And when the farmers, the men and women who were in the audience she addressed—when they went to Bismarck where the trial was held to testify in her favor, to swear that she had not used the language she was charged with having used, the judge refused to allow them to go upon the stand. This would seem incredible to me if I had not had some experience of my own with federal courts.

Who appoints our federal judges? The people? In all the history of the country, the working class have never named a federal judge. There are 121 of these judges and every solitary one holds his position, his tenure, through the influence and power of corporate capital. The corporations and trusts dictate their appointment. And when they go to the bench, they go, not to serve, the people, but to serve the interests that place them and keep them where they are.

Why, the other day, by a vote of five to four—a kind of craps game— come seven, come 'leven —they declared the child labor law unconstitutional—a law secured after twenty years of education and agitation on the part of all kinds of people. And yet, by a majority of one, the Supreme Court a body of corporation lawyers, with just one exception, wiped that law from the statute books, and this in our so-called democracy, so that we may continue to grind the flesh and blood and bones of puny little children into profits for the Junkers of Wall Street. And this in a country that boasts of fighting to make the world safe for democracy! The history of this country is being written in the blood of the childhood the industrial lords have murdered.

These are not palatable truths to them. They do not like to hear them; and what is more they do not want you to hear them. And that is why they brand us as undesirable citizens, and as disloyalists and traitors. If we were actual traitors—traitors to the people and to their welfare and progress, we would be regarded as eminently respectable citizens of the republic; we would hold high office, have princely incomes, and ride in limousines; and we would be pointed out as the elect who have succeeded in life in honorable pursuit, and worthy of emulation by the youth of the land. It is precisely because we are disloyal to the traitors that we are loyal to the people of this nation.

Scott Nearing! You have heard of Scott Nearing. He is the greatest teacher in the United States. He was in the University of Pennsylvania until the Board of Trustees, consisting of great capitalists, captains of industry, found that he was teaching sound economics to the students in his classes. This sealed his fate in that institution. They sneeringly charged—just as the same usurers, money-changers, pharisees, hypocrites charged the Judean Carpenter some twenty centuries ago—that he was a false teacher and that he was stirring up the people.

The Man of Galilee, the Carpenter, the workingman who became the revolutionary agitator of his day soon found himself to be an undesirable citizen in the eyes of the ruling knaves and they had him crucified. And now their lineal descendants say of Scott Nearing, "He is preaching false economics. We cannot crucify him as we did his elder brother but we can deprive him of employment and so cut off his income and starve him to death or into submission. We will not only discharge him but place his name upon the blacklist and make it impossible for him to earn a living. He is a dangerous man for he is teaching the truth and opening the eyes of the people." And the truth, oh, the truth has always been unpalatable and intolerable to the class who live out of the sweat and misery of the working class.

Max Eastman has been indicted and his paper suppressed, just as the papers with which I have been connected have all been suppressed. What a wonderful compliment they pay us! They are afraid that we may mislead and contaminate you. You are their wards; they are your guardians and they know what is best for you to read and hear and know. They are bound to see to it that our vicious doctrines do not reach your ears. And so in our great democracy, under our free institutions, they flatter our press by suppression; and they ignorantly imagine that they have silenced revolutionary propaganda in the United States. What an awful mistake they make for our benefit! As a matter of justice to them we should respond with resolutions of thanks and gratitude. Thousands of people who had never before heard of our papers are now inquiring for and insisting upon seeing them. They have succeeded only in arousing curiosity in our literature and propaganda. And woe to him who reads Socialist literature from curiosity! He is surely a goner. I have known of a thousand experiments but never one that failed . . .

How stupid and shortsighted the ruling class really is! Cupidity is stone blind. It has no vision. The greedy, profit-seeking exploiter cannot see beyond the end of his nose. He can see a chance for an "opening"; he is cunning enough to know what graft is and where it is, and how it can be secured, but vision he has none—not the slightest. He knows nothing of the great throbbing world that spreads out in all directions. He has no capacity for literature; no appreciation of art; no soul for beauty. That is the penalty the parasites pay for the violation of the laws of life. The Rockefellers are blind. Every move they make in their game of greed but hastens their own doom. Every blow they strike at the Socialist movement reacts upon themselves. Every time they strike at us they hit themselves. It never fails. Every time they strangle a Socialist paper they add a thousand voices proclaiming the truth of the principles of socialism and the ideals of the Socialist movement. They help us in spite of themselves . . .

Yes, my comrades, my heart is attuned to yours. Aye, all our hearts now throb as one great heart responsive to the battle cry of the social revolution. Here, in this alert and inspiring assemblage our hearts are with the Bolsheviki of Russia. Those heroic men and women, those unconquerable comrades have by their incomparable valor and sacrifice added fresh luster to the fame of the international movement. Those Russian comrades of ours have made greater sacrifices, have suffered more, and have shed more heroic blood than any like number of men and women anywhere on earth; they have laid the foundation of the first real democracy that ever drew the breath of life in this world. And the very first act of the triumphant Russian revolution was to proclaim a state of peace with all mankind, coupled with a fervent moral appeal, not to kings, not to emperors, rulers or diplomats but to the people of all nations. Here we have the very breath of democracy, the quintessence of the dawning freedom. The Russian revolution proclaimed its glorious triumph in its ringing and inspiring appeal to the peoples of all the earth. In a humane and fraternal spirit new Russia, emancipated at last from the curse of the centuries, called upon all nations engaged in the frightful war, the Central Powers as well as the Allies, to send representatives to a conference to lay down terms of peace that should be just and lasting. Here was the supreme opportunity to strike the blow to make the world safe for democracy. Was there any response to that noble appeal that in some day to come will be written in letters of gold in the history of the world? Was there any response whatever to that appeal for universal peace? No, not the slightest attention was paid to it by the Christian nations engaged in the terrible slaughter.

It has been charged that Lenin and Trotsky and the leaders of the revolution were treacherous, that they made a traitorous peace with Germany. Let us consider that proposition briefly. At the time of the revolution Russia had been three years in the war. Under the Czar she had lost more than four million of her ill-clad, poorly-equipped, half-starved soldiers, slain outright or disabled on the field of battle. She was absolutely bankrupt. Her soldiers were mainly without arms. This was what was bequeathed to the revolution by the Czar and his regime; and for this condition Lenin and Trotsky were not responsible, nor the Bolsheviki. For this appalling state of affairs the Czar and his rotten bureaucracy were solely responsible. When the Bolsheviki came into power and went through the archives they found and exposed the secret treaties—the treaties that were made between the Czar and the French government, the British government and the Italian government, proposing, after the victory was achieved, to dismember the German Empire and destroy the Central Powers. These treaties have never been denied nor repudiated. Very little has been said about them in the American press. I have a copy of these treaties, showing that the purpose of the Allies is exactly the purpose of the Central Powers, and that is the conquest and spoilation of the weaker nations that has always been the purpose of war.

Wars throughout history have been waged for conquest and plunder. In the Middle Ages when the feudal lords who inhabited the castles whose towers may still be seen along the Rhine concluded to enlarge their domains, to increase their power, their prestige and their wealth they declared war upon one another. But they themselves did not go to war any more than the modern feudal lords, the barons of Wall Street go to war. The feudal barons of the Middle Ages, the economic predecessors of the capitalists of our day, declared all wars. And their miserable serfs fought all the battles. The poor, ignorant serfs had been taught to revere their masters; to believe that when their masters declared war upon one another, it was their patriotic duty to fall upon one another and to cut one another's throats for the profit and glory of the lords and barons who held them in contempt. And that is war in a nutshell. The master class has always declared the wars; the subject class has always fought the battles. The master class has had all to gain and nothing to lose, while the subject class has had nothing to gain and all to lose—especially their lives.

They have always taught and trained you to believe it to be your patriotic duty to go to war and to have yourselves slaughtered at their command. But in all the history of the world you, the people, have never had a voice in declaring war, and strange as it certainly appears, no war by any nation in any age has ever been declared by the people.

And here let me emphasize the fact—and it cannot be repeated too often —that the working class who fight all the battles, the working class who make the supreme sacrifices, the working class who freely shed their blood and furnish the corpses, have never yet had a voice in either declaring war or making peace. It is the ruling class that invariably does both. They alone declare war and they alone make peace.

> Yours not to reason why;
> Yours but to do and die.

That is their motto and we object on the part of the awakening workers of this nation.

If war is right let it be declared by the people. You who have your lives to lose, you certainly

The heart of the international Socialist never beats a retreat.

They are pressing forward, here, there and everywhere, in all the zones that girdle the globe. Everywhere these awakening workers, these class-conscious proletarians, these hardy sons and daughters of honest toil are proclaiming the glad tidings of the coming emancipation, everywhere their hearts are attuned to the most sacred cause that ever challenged men and women to action in all the history of the world. Everywhere they are moving toward democracy and the dawn; marching toward the sunrise, their faces all aglow with the light of the coming day. These are the Socialists, the most zealous and enthusiastic crusaders the world has ever known. They are making history that will light up the horizon of coming generations, for their mission is the emancipation of the human race. They have been reviled; they have been ridiculed, persecuted, imprisoned and have suffered death, but they have been sufficient to themselves and their cause, and their final triumph is but a question of time.

Do you wish to hasten the day of victory? Join the Socialist Party! Don't wait for the morrow. Join now! Enroll your name without fear and take your place where you belong. You cannot do your duty by proxy. You have got to do it yourself and do it squarely and then as you look yourself in the face you will have no occasion to blush. You will know what it is to be a real man or woman. You will lose nothing; you will gain everything. Not only will you lose nothing but you will find something of infinite value, and that something will be yourself. And that is your supreme need—to find yourself—to really know yourself and your purpose in life.

You need at this time especially to know that you are fit for something better than slavery and cannon fodder. You need to know that you were not created to work and produce and impoverish yourself to enrich an idle exploiter. You need to know that you have a mind to improve, a soul to develop, and a manhood to sustain . . .

To turn your back on the corrupt Republican Party and the still more corrupt Democratic Party—the gold-dust lackeys of the ruling class counts for still more after you have stepped out of those popular and corrupt capitalist parties to join a minority party that has an ideal, that stands for a principle, and fights for a cause. This will be the most important change you have ever made and the time will come when you will thank me for having made the suggestion. It was the day of days for me. I remember it well. It was like passing from midnight darkness to the noontide light of day. It came almost like a flash and found me ready. It must have been in such a flash that great, seething, throbbing Russia, prepared by centuries of slavery and tears and martyrdom, was transformed from a dark continent to a land of living light . . .

In the Republican and Democratic parties you of the common herd are not expected to think. That is not only unnecessary but might lead you astray. That is what the "intellectual" leaders are for. They do the thinking and you do the voting. They ride in carriages at the front where the band plays and you tramp in the mud, bringing up the rear with great enthusiasm.

The capitalist system affects to have great regard and reward for intellect, and the capitalists give themselves full credit for having superior brains. When we have ventured to say that the time would come when the working class would rule they have bluntly answered "Never! it requires brains to rule." The workers of course have none. And they certainly try hard to prove it by proudly supporting the political parties of their masters under whose administration they are kept in poverty and servitude . . .

They are continually talking about your patriotic duty. It is not their but your patriotic duty that they are concerned about. There is a decided difference. Their patriotic duty never takes them to the firing line or chucks them into the trenches.

And now among other things they are urging you to "cultivate" war gardens, while at the same time a government war report just issued shows that practically 52 percent of the arable, tillable soil is held out of use by the landlords, speculators and profiteers. They themselves do not cultivate the soil. They could not if they would. Nor do they allow others to cultivate it. They keep it idle to enrich themselves, to pocket the millions of dollars of unearned increment. Who is it that makes this land valuable while it is fenced in and kept out of use? It is the people. Who pockets this tremendous accumulation of value? The landlords. And these landlords who toil not and spin not are supreme among American "patriots."

In passing I suggest that we stop a moment to think about the term "landlord." "LANDLORD!" Lord of the Land! The lord of the land is indeed a superpatriot. This lord who practically owns the earth tells you that we are fighting this war to make the world safe for democracy—he who shuts out all humanity from his private domain; he who profiteers at the expense of the people who have been slain and mutilated by multiplied thousands, under pretense of being the great American patriot. It is he, this identical patriot who is in fact the archenemy of the people; it is he that you need to wipe from power. It is he who is a far greater menace to your liberty and your well-being than the Prussian Junkers on the other side of the Atlantic ocean.

Fifty-two percent of the land kept out of use, according to their own figures! They tell you that there is an alarming shortage of flour and that you need to produce more. They tell you further that you have got to save wheat so that more can be exported for the soldiers who are fighting on the other side, while half of your tillable soil is held out of use by the landlords and profiteers. What do you think of that? . . .

Lincoln said: "If you want that thing that is the thing you want"; and you will get it to your heart's content. But some good day you will wake up and realize that a change is needed and wonder why you did not know it long before. Yes, a change is certainly needed, not merely a change of party but a change of system; a change from slavery to freedom and from despotism to democracy, wide as the world. When this change comes at last, we shall rise from brutehood to brotherhood, and to accomplish it we have to educate and organize the workers industrially and politically, but not along the zigzag craft lines laid down by Gompers, who through all of his career has favored the master class. You never hear the capitalist press speak of him nowadays except in praise and adulation. He has recently come into great prominence as a patriot. You never find him on the unpopular side of a great issue. He is always conservative, satisfied to leave the labor problem to be settled finally at the banqueting board with Elihu Root, Andrew Carnegie and the rest of the plutocratic civic federationists. When they drink wine and smoke scab cigars together the labor question is settled so far as they are concerned . . .

When we unite and act together on the industrial field and when we vote together on election day we shall develop the supreme power of the one class that can and will bring permanent peace to the world. We shall then have the intelligence, the courage and the power for our great task. In due time industry will be organized on a cooperative basis. We shall conquer the public power. We shall then transfer the title deeds of the railroads, the telegraph lines, the mines, mills and great industries to the people in their collective capacity; we shall take possession of all these social utilities in the name of the people. We shall then have industrial democracy. We shall be a free nation whose government is of and by and for the people.

And now for all of us to do our duty! The clarion call is ringing in our ears and we cannot falter without being convicted of treason to ourselves and to our great cause.

Do not worry over the charge of treason to your masters, but be concerned about the treason that involves yourselves. Be true to yourself and you cannot be a traitor to any good cause on earth.

Yes, in good time we are going to sweep into power in this nation and throughout the world. We are going to destroy all enslaving and degrading capitalist institutions and re-create them as free and humanizing institutions. The world is daily changing before our eyes. The sun of capitalism is setting; the sun of socialism is rising. It is our duty to build the new nation and the free republic. We need industrial and social builders. We Socialists are the builders of the beautiful world that is to be. We are all pledged to do our part. We are inviting—aye challenging you this afternoon in the name of your own manhood and womanhood to join us and do your part.

In due time the hour will strike and this great cause triumphant—the greatest in history—will proclaim the emancipation of the working class and the brotherhood of all mankind.

Source: Eugene V. Debs, The Canton, Ohio Anti-War Speech (Excerpts). June 16, 1918. (https://www.marxists.org/archive/debs/works/1918/canton. htm. Accessed April 9, 2016).

DOCUMENT 5

Schenck v. United States (1919)

MR. JUSTICE HOLMES delivered the opinion of the court. This is an indictment in three counts. The first charges a conspiracy to violate the Espionage Act of June 15, 1917, c. 30, § 3, 40 Stat. 217, 219, by causing and attempting to cause insubordination, &c., in the military and naval forces of the United States, and to obstruct the recruiting and enlistment service of the United States, when the United States was at war with the German Empire, to-wit, that the defendants willfully conspired to have printed and circulated to men who had been called and accepted for military service under the Act of May 18, 1917, a document set forth and alleged to be calculated to cause such insubordination and obstruction. The count alleges overt acts in pursuance of the conspiracy, ending in the distribution of the document set forth. The second count alleges a conspiracy to commit an offence against the United States, to-wit, to use the mails for the transmission of matter declared to be nonmailable by Title XII, § 2 of the Act of June 15, 1917, to-wit, the above mentioned document, with an averment of the same overt acts. The third count charges an unlawful use of the mails for the transmission of the same matter and otherwise as above. The defendants were found guilty on all the counts. They set up the First Amendment to the Constitution forbidding Congress to make any law abridging the freedom of speech, or of the press, and bringing the case here on that ground have argued some other points also of which we must dispose.

It is argued that the evidence, if admissible, was not sufficient to prove that the defendant Schenck was concerned in sending the documents. According to the testimony, Schenck said he was general secretary of the Socialist party, and had charge of the Socialist headquarters from which the documents were sent. He identified a book found there as the minutes of the Executive Committee of the party. The book showed a resolution of August 13, 1917, that 15,000 leaflets should be printed on the other side of one of them in use, to be mailed to men who had passed exemption boards, and for distribution. Schenck personally attended to the printing. On August 20, the general secretary's report said "Obtained new leaflets from printer and started work addressing envelopes" &c., and there was a resolve that Comrade Schenck be allowed $125 for sending leaflets through the mail. He said that he had about fifteen or sixteen thousand printed. There were files of the circular in question in the inner office which he said were printed on the other side of the one sided circular, and were there for distribution. Other copies were proved to have been sent through the mails to drafted men. Without going into confirmatory details that were proved, no reasonable man could doubt that the defendant Schenck was largely instrumental in sending the circulars about. As to the defendant Baer, there was evidence that she was a member of the Executive Board, and that the minutes of its transactions were hers. The argument as to the sufficiency of the evidence that the defendants conspired to send the documents only impairs the seriousness of the real defence.

It is objected that the documentary evidence was not admissible because obtained upon a search warrant, valid so far as appears. The contrary is established. *Adams v. New York*, 192 U.S. 585; *Weeks v. United States*, 232 U.S. 383, 395, 396. The search warrant did not issue against the defendant, but against the Socialist headquarters at 1326 Arch Street, and it would seem that the documents technically were not even in the defendants' possession. *See Johnson v. United States*, 228 U.S. 457. Notwithstanding some protest in argument, the notion that evidence even directly proceeding from the defendant in a criminal proceeding is excluded in all cases by the Fifth Amendment is plainly unsound. *Holt v. United States*, 218 U.S. 245, 252, 253.

The document in question, upon its first printed side, recited the first section of the Thirteenth Amendment, said that the idea embodied in it was violated by the Conscription Act, and that a conscript is little better than a convict. In impassioned language, it intimated that conscription was despotism in its worst form, and a monstrous wrong against humanity in the interest of Wall Street's chosen few. It said "Do not submit to intimidation," but in form, at least, confined itself to peaceful measures such as a petition for the repeal of the act. The other and later printed side of the sheet was headed "Assert Your Rights." It stated reasons for alleging that anyone violated the Constitution when he refused to recognize "your right to assert your opposition to the draft," and went on If you do not assert and support your rights, you are helping to deny or disparage rights which it is the solemn duty of all citizens and residents of the United States to retain.

It described the arguments on the other side as coming from cunning politicians and a mercenary capitalist press, and even silent consent to the conscription law as helping to support an infamous conspiracy. It denied the power to send our citizens away to foreign shores to shoot up the people of other lands, and added that words could not express the condemnation such cold-blooded ruthlessness deserves, &c., &c., winding up, "You must do your share to maintain, support and uphold the rights of the people of this country." Of course, the document would not have been sent unless it had been intended to have some effect, and we do not see what effect it could be expected to have upon persons subject to the draft except to influence them to obstruct the carrying of it out. The defendants do not deny that the jury might find against them on this point.

But it is said, suppose that that was the tendency of this circular, it is protected by the First Amendment to the Constitution. Two of the strongest expressions are said to be quoted respectively from well known public men. It well may be that the prohibition of laws abridging the freedom of speech is not confined to previous restraints, although to prevent them may have been the main purpose, as intimated in *Patterson v. Colorado*, 205 U.S. 454, 462. We admit that, in many places and in ordinary times, the defendants, in saying all that was said in the circular, would have been within their constitutional rights. But the character of every act depends upon the circumstances in which it is done. *Aikens v. Wisconsin*, 195 U.S. 194, 205, 206. The most stringent protection of free speech would not protect a man in falsely shouting fire in a theatre and causing a panic. It does not even protect a man from an injunction against uttering words that may have all the effect of force. *Gompers v. Bucks Stove & Range Co.*, 221 U.S. 418, 439. The question in every case is whether the words used are used in such circumstances and are of such a nature as to create a clear and present danger that they will bring about the substantive evils that Congress has a right to prevent. It is a question of proximity and degree. When a nation is at war, many things that might be said in time of peace are such a hindrance to its effort that their utterance will not be endured so long as men fight, and that no Court could regard them as protected by any constitutional right. It seems to be admitted that, if an actual obstruction of the recruiting service were proved, liability for words that produced that effect might be enforced. The statute of 1917, in § 4, punishes conspiracies to obstruct, as well as actual obstruction. If the act (speaking, or circulating a paper), its tendency, and the intent with which it is done are the same, we perceive no ground for saying that success alone warrants making the act a crime. *Goldman v. United States*, 245 U.S. 474, 477. Indeed, that case might be said to dispose of the present contention if the precedent covers all *media concludendi*. But, as the right to free speech was not referred to specially, we have thought fit to add a few words.

It was not argued that a conspiracy to obstruct the draft was not within the words of the Act of 1917. The words are "obstruct the recruiting or enlistment service," and it might be suggested that they refer only to making it hard to get volunteers. Recruiting heretofore usually having been accomplished by getting volunteers, the word is apt to call up that method only in our minds. But recruiting is gaining fresh supplies for the forces, as well by draft as otherwise. It is put as an alternative to enlistment or voluntary enrollment in this act. The fact that the Act of 1917 was enlarged by the amending Act of May 16, 1918, c. 75, 40 Stat. 553, of course, does not affect the present indictment, and would not even if the former act had been repealed. Rev.Stats., § 13.

Judgments affirmed.

Source: *Schenck v. United States* (249 U.S. 47, 1919).

DOCUMENT 6

Abrams v. United States (1919)

Mr. Justice CLARKE delivered the opinion of the Court.

On a single indictment, containing four counts, the five plaintiffs in error, hereinafter designated the defendants, were convicted of conspiring to violate provisions of the [250 U.S. 616, 617] Espionage Act of Congress (section 3, title I, of Act June 15, 1917, c. 30, 40 Stat. 219, as amended by Act May 16, 1918, c. 75, 40 Stat. 553 [Comp. St. 1918, 10212c]).

Each of the first three counts charged the defendants with conspiring, when the United States was at war with the Imperial Government of Germany, to unlawfully utter, print, write and publish: In the first count, 'disloyal, scurrilous and abusive language about the form of government of the United States;' in the second count, language 'intended to bring the form of government of the United States into contempt, scorn, contumely, and disrepute;' and in the third count, language 'intended to incite, provoke and encourage resistance to the United States in said war.' The charge in the fourth count was that the defendants conspired 'when the United States was at war with the Imperial German Government, ... unlawfully and willfully, by utterance, writing, printing and publication to urge, incite and advocate curtailment of production of things and products, to wit, ordnance and ammunition, necessary and essential to the prosecution of the war.' The offenses were charged in the language of the act of Congress.

It was charged in each count of the indictment that it was a part of the conspiracy that the defendants would attempt to accomplish their unlawful purpose by printing, writing and distributing in the city of New York many copies of a leaflet or circular, printed in the English language, and of another printed in the Yiddish language, copies of which, properly identified, were attached to the indictment.

All of the five defendants were born in Russia. They were intelligent, had considerable schooling, and at the time they were arrested they had lived in the United States terms varying from five to ten years, but none of them had applied for naturalization. Four of them testified as witnesses in their own behalf, and of these three frankly avowed that they were 'rebels,' 'revolutionists,' [250 U.S. 616, 618] 'anarchists,' that they did not believe in government in any form, and they declared that they had no interest whatever in the government of the United States. The fourth defendant testified that he was a 'Socialist' and believed in 'a proper kind of government, not capitalistic,' but in his classification the government of the United States was 'capitalistic.'

It was admitted on the trial that the defendants had united to print and distribute the described circulars and that 5,000 of them had been printed and distributed about the 22d day of August, 1918. The group had a meeting place in New York City, in rooms rented by defendant Abrams, under an assumed name, and there the subject of printing the circulars was discussed about two weeks before the defendants were arrested. The defendant Abrams, although not a printer, on July 27, 1918, purchased the printing outfit with which the circulars were printed, and installed it in a basement room where the work was done at night. The circulars were distributed, some by throwing them from a window of a building where one of the defendants was employed and others secretly, in New York City.

The defendants pleaded 'not guilty,' and the case of the government consisted in showing the facts we have stated, and in introducing in evidence copies of the two printed circulars attached to the indictment, a sheet entitled 'Revolutionists Unite for Action,' written by the defendant Lipman, and found on him when he was arrested, and another paper, found at the headquarters of the group, and for which Abrams assumed responsibility.

Thus the conspiracy and the doing of the overt acts charged were largely admitted and were fully established.

On the record thus described it is argued, somewhat faintly, that the acts charged against the defendants were not unlawful because within the protection of that freedom [250 U.S. 616, 619] of speech and of the press which is guaranteed by the First Amendment to the Constitution of the United States, and that the entire Espionage Act is unconstitutional because in conflict with that amendment. . .

The first of the two articles attached to the indictment is conspicuously headed, 'The Hypocrisy of the United States and her Allies.' After denouncing President Wilson as a hypocrite and a coward because troops were sent into Russia, it proceeds to assail our government in general, saying: [250 U.S. 616, 620] 'His [the President's] shameful, cowardly silence about the intervention in Russia reveals the hypocrisy of the plutocratic gang in Washington and vicinity.'

It continues:

'He [the President] is too much of a coward to come out openly and say: "We capitalistic nations cannot afford to have a proletarian republic in Russia."'

Among the capitalistic nations Abrams testified the United States was included.

Growing more inflammatory as it proceeds, the circular culminates in:

'The Russian Revolution cries: Workers of the World! Awake! Rise! Put down your enemy and mine!'

'Yes friends, there is only one enemy of the workers of the world and that is CAPITALISM.'

This is clearly an appeal to the 'workers' of this country to arise and put down by force the government of the United States which they characterize as their 'hypocritical,' 'cowardly' and 'capitalistic' enemy.

It concludes:

'Awake! Awake, you Workers of the World!
REVOLUTIONISTS.'

The second of the articles was printed in the Yiddish language and in the translation is headed, 'Workers-Wake Up.' After referring to 'his Majesty, Mr. Wilson, and the rest of the gang, dogs of all colors!' it continues:

'Workers, Russian emigrants, you who had the least belief in the honesty of our government,'—which defendants admitted referred to the United States government—'must now throw away all confidence, must spit in the face the false, hypocritic, military propaganda which has fooled you so relentlessly, calling forth your sympathy, your help, to the prosecution of the war.'

The purpose of this obviously was to persuade the persons to whom it was addressed to turn a deaf ear to patriotic [250 U.S. 616, 621] appeals in behalf of the government of the United States, and to cease to render it assistance in the prosecution of the war.

It goes on:

'With the money which you have loaned, or are going to loan them, they will make bullets not only for the Germans, but also for the Workers Soviets of Russia. Workers in the ammunition factories, you are producing bullets, bayonets, cannon, to murder not only the Germans, but also your dearest, best, who are in Russia and are fighting for freedom.'

It will not do to say, as is now argued, that the only intent of these defendants was to prevent injury to the Russian cause. Men must be held to have intended, and to be accountable for, the effects which their acts were likely to produce. Even if their primary purpose and intent was to aid the cause of the Russian Revolution, the plan of action which they adopted necessarily involved, before it could be realized, defeat of the war program of the United States, for the obvious effect of this appeal, if it should become effective, as they hoped it might, would be to persuade persons of character such as those whom they regarded themselves as addressing, not to aid government loans and not to work in ammunition factories, where their work would produce 'bullets, bayonets, cannon' and other munitions of war, the use of which would cause the 'murder' of Germans and Russians.

Again, the spirit becomes more bitter as it proceeds to declare that—

'America and her Allies have betrayed [the Workers]. Their robberish aims are clear to all men. The destruction of the Russian Revolution, that is the politics of the march to Russia.'
    'Workers, our reply to the barbaric intervention has to be a general strike! An open challenge only will let the government know that not only the Russian Worker fights for [250 U.S. 616, 622] freedom, but also here in America lives the spirit of Revolution.'

This is not an attempt to bring about a change of administration by candid discussion, for no matter what may have incited the outbreak on the part of the defendant anarchists, the manifest purpose of such a publication was to create an attempt to defeat the war plans of the government of the United States, by bringing upon the country the paralysis of a general strike, thereby arresting the production of all munitions and other things essential to the conduct of the war.

This purpose is emphasized in the next paragraph, which reads:

'Do not let the government scare you with their wild punishment in prisons, hanging and shooting. We must not and will not betray the splendid fighters of Russia. Workers, up to fight.'

After more of the same kind, the circular concludes:

'Woe unto those who will be in the way of progress. Let solidarity live!'
    It is signed, 'The Rebels.'
    That the interpretation we have put upon these articles, circulated in the greatest port of our land, from which great numbers of soldiers were at the time taking ship daily, and in which great quantities of war supplies of every kind were at the time being manufactured for transportation overseas, is not only the fair interpretation of them, but that it is the meaning which their

authors consciously intended should be conveyed by them to others is further shown by the additional writings found in the meeting place of the defendant group and on the person of one of them. One of these circulars is headed: 'Revolutionists! Unite for Action!'

After denouncing the President as 'Our Kaiser' and the hypocrisy of the United States and her Allies, this article concludes: [250 U.S. 616, 623] 'Socialists, Anarchists, Industrial Workers of the World, Socialists, Labor party men and other revolutionary organizations Unite for Action and let us save the Workers' Republic of Russia!

'Know you lovers of freedom that in order to save the Russian revolution, we must keep the armies of the allied countries busy at home.'

Thus was again avowed the purpose to throw the country into a state of revolution, if possible, and to thereby frustrate the military program of the government.

The remaining article, after denouncing the President for what is characterized as hostility to the Russian revolution, continues:

'We, the toilers of America, who believe in real liberty, shall pledge ourselves, in case the United States will participate in that bloody conspiracy against Russia, to create so great a disturbance that the autocrats of America shall be compelled to keep their armies at home, and not be able to spare any for Russia.'

It concludes with this definite threat of armed rebellion:

'If they will use arms against the Russian people to enforce their standard of order, so will we use arms, and they shall never see the ruin of the Russian Revolution.'

These excerpts sufficiently show, that while the immediate occasion for this particular outbreak of lawlessness, on the part of the defendant alien anarchists, may have been resentment caused by our government sending troops into Russia as a strategic operation against the Germans on the eastern battle front, yet the plain purpose of their propaganda was to excite, at the supreme crisis of the war, disaffection, sedition, riots, and, as they hoped, revolution, in this country for the purpose of embarrassing and if possible defeating the military plans of the government in Europe. A technical distinction may perhaps be taken between disloyal and abusive language applied to the form of our government or language intended to bring the form [250 U.S. 616, 624] of our government into contempt and disrepute, and language of like character and intended to produce like results directed against the President and Congress, the agencies through which that form of government must function in time of war. But it is not necessary to a decision of this case to consider whether such distinction is vital or merely formal, for the language of these circulars was obviously intended to provoke and to encourage resistance to the United States in the war, as the third count runs, and, the defendants, in terms, plainly urged and advocated a resort to a general strike of workers in ammunition factories for the purpose of curtailing the production of ordnance and munitions necessary and essential to the prosecution of the war as is charged in the fourth count. Thus it is clear not only that some evidence but that much persuasive evidence was before the jury tending to prove that the defendants were guilty as charged in both the third and fourth counts of the indictment and under the long established rule of law hereinbefore stated the judgment of the District Court must be

AFFIRMED.

Source: *Abrams v. United States* (250 U.S. 616, 1919).

Warren Harding Campaign Speech, *Back to Normal* Before the Home Market Club, Boston, Massachusetts

Warren G. Harding

May 14, 1920

*T*here isn't anything the matter with the world's civilization except that humanity is viewing it through a vision impaired in a cataclysmal war. Poise has been disturbed and nerves have been racked, and fever has rendered men irrational; sometimes there have been draughts upon the dangerous cup of barbarity and men have wandered far from safe paths, but the human procession still marches in the right direction.

Here, in the United States, we feel the reflex, rather than the hurting wound, but we still think straight, and we mean to act straight, and mean to hold firmly to all that was ours when war involved us, and seek the higher attainments which are the only compensations that so supreme a tragedy may give mankind.

America's present need is not heroics, but healing; not nostrums, but normalcy; not revolution, but restoration; not agitation, but adjustment; not surgery, but serenity; not the dramatic, but the dispassionate; not experiment, but equipoise; not submergence in internationality, but sustainment in triumphant nationality. It is one thing to battle successfully against world domination by military autocracy, because the infinite God never intended such a program, but it is quite another thing to revise human nature and suspend the fundamental laws of life and all of life's acquirements.

The world called for peace, and has its precarious variety. America demands peace, formal as well as actual, and means to have it, regardless of political exigencies and campaign issues. If it must be a campaign issue, we shall have peace and discuss it afterward, because the actuality is imperative, and the theory is only illusive. Then we may set our own house in order. We challenged the proposal that an armed autocrat should dominate the world; it ill becomes us to assume that a rhetorical autocrat shall direct all humanity.

This republic has its ample tasks. If we put an end to false economics which lure humanity to utter chaos, ours will be the commanding example of world leadership today. If we can prove a representative popular government under which a citizenship seeks what it may do for the government rather than what the government may do for individuals, we shall do more to make democracy safe for the world than all armed conflict ever recorded. The world needs to be reminded that all human ills are not curable by legislation, and that quantity of statutory enactment and excess of government offer no substitute for quality of citizenship.

The problems of maintained civilization are not to be solved by a transfer of responsibility from citizenship to government, and no eminent page in history was ever drafted by the standards of mediocrity. More, no government is worthy of the name which is directed by influence on the one hand, or moved by intimidation on the other.

Nothing is more vital to this republic to-day than clear and intelligent understanding. Men must understand one another, and government and men must understand each other. For emergence from the wreckage of war, for the clarification of fevered minds, we must all give and take, we must both sympathize and inspire, but must learn griefs and aspirations, we must seek the common grounds of mutuality.

There can be no disguising everlasting truths. Speak it plainly, no people ever recovered from the distressing waste of war except through work and denial. There is no other way. We shall make no recovery in seeking how little men can do, our restoration lies in doing the most which is reasonably possible for individuals to do. Under production and hateful profiteering are both morally criminal, and must be combated. America can not be content with minimums of production to-day, the crying need is maximums. If we may have maximums of production we shall have minimums of cost, and profiteering will be speeded to its deserved punishment. Money values are not destroyed, they are temporarily distorted. War wasted hundreds of billions, and depleted world store-houses, and cultivated new demands, and it hardened selfishness and gave awakening touch to elemental greed. Humanity needs renewed consecrations to what we call fellow citizenship.

Out of the supreme tragedy must come a new order and a higher order, and I gladly acclaim it. But war has not abolished work, has not established the processes of seizure or the rule of physical might. Nor has it provided a governmental panacea for human ills, or the magic touch that makes failure a success. Indeed, it has revealed no new reward for idleness, no substitute for the sweat of a man's face in the contest for subsistence and acquirement.

There is no new appraisal for the supremacy of law. That is a thing surpassing and eternal. A contempt for international law wrought the supreme tragedy, contempt for our national and state laws will rend the glory of the republic, and failure to abide the proven laws of to-day's civilization will lead to temporary chaos.

No one need doubt the ultimate result, because immutable laws have challenged the madness of all experiment. But we are living to-day, and it is ours to save ourselves from colossal blunder and its excessive penalty.

My best judgment of America's needs is to steady down, to get squarely on our feet, to make sure of the right path. Let's get out of the fevered delirium of war, with the hallucination that all the money in the world is to be made in the madness of war and the wildness of its aftermath. Let us stop to consider that tranquility at home is more precious than peace abroad, and that both our good fortune and our eminence are dependent on the normal forward stride of all the American people.

Nothing is so imperative to-day as efficient production and efficient transportation, to adjust the balances in our own transactions and to hold our place in the activities of the world. The relation of real values is little altered by the varying coins of exchange, and that American is blind to actualities who thinks we can add to cost of production without impairing our hold in world markets. Our part is more than to hold, we must add to what we have.

It is utter folly to talk about reducing the cost of living without restored and increased efficiency or production on the one hand and more prudent consumption on the other. No law will work the miracle. Only the American people themselves can solve the situation. There must be the conscience of capital in omitting profiteering, there must be the conscience of labor in efficiently producing, there must be a public conscience in restricting outlay and promoting thrift.

Sober capital must make appeal to intoxicated wealth, and thoughtful labor must appeal to the radical who has no thought of the morrow, to effect the needed understanding. Exacted profits, because the golden stream is flooding, and pyramided wages to meet a mounting cost that must be halted, will speed us to disaster just as sure as the morrow comes, and we ought to think soberly and avoid it. We ought to dwell in the heights of good fortune for a generation to come, and I pray that we will, but we need a benediction of wholesome common sense to give us that assurance.

I pray for sober thinking in behalf of the future of America. No worth-while republic ever went the tragic way to destruction, which did not begin the downward course through luxury of life and extravagance of living. More, the simple living and thrifty people will be the first to recover from a war's waste and all its burdens, and our people ought to be the first recovered. Herein is greater opportunity than lies in alliance, compact or super-government. It is America's chance to lead in example and prove to the world the reign of reason in representative popular government where people think who assume to rule.

No overall fad will quicken our thoughtfulness. We might try repairs on the old clothes and simplicity for the new. I know the tendency to wish the thing denied, I know the human hunger for a new thrill, but denial enhances the ultimate satisfaction, and stabilizes our indulgence. A blasé people is the unhappiest in all the world.

It seems to me singularly appropriate to address this membership an additional word about production. I believe most cordially in the home market first for the American product. There is no other way to assure our prosperity. I rejoice in our normal capacity to consume our rational, health-ful consumption.

We have protected our home market with war's barrage. But the barrage has lifted with the passing of the war. The American people will not heed to-day, because world competition is not yet restored, but the morrow will soon come when the world will seek our markets and our trade balances, and we must think of America first or surrender our eminence.

The thought is not selfish. We want to share with the world in seeking becoming restoration. But peoples will trade and seek wealth in their exchanges, and every conflict in the adjustment of peace was founded on the hope of promoting trade conditions. I heard expressed, before the Foreign Relations Committee of the Senate, the aspirations of nationality and the hope of commerce to develop and expand aspiring peoples. Knowing that those two thoughts are inspiring all humanity, as they have since civilization began, I can only marvel at the American who consents to surrender either. There may be conscience, humanity and justice in both, and without them the glory of the republic is done. I want to go on, secure and unafraid, holding fast to the American inheritance and confident of the supreme American fulfillment.

Source: Warren G. Harding, Campaign Speech *Back to Normal* before the Home Market Club, Boston, Massachusetts. (May 14, 1920). (http://live-fromthetrail.com/about-the-book/speeches/chapter-3/senator-warren-g-harding. Accessed February 15, 2016).

DOCUMENT 8

Gitlow v. People of State of New York (1925)

Mr. Justice SANFORD delivered the opinion of the Court.

Benjamin Gitlow was indicted in the Supreme Court of New York, with three others, for the statutory crime of criminal anarchy. New York Penal Law, 160, 161.1 He was separately tried, convicted, and sentenced to imprisonment. The judgment was affirmed by the Appellate Division and by the Court of Appeals. People v. Gitlow, 195 App. Div. 773, 187 N. Y. S. 783; 234 N. Y. 132, 136 N. E. 317; and 234 N. Y. 529, 138 N. E. 438. The case is here on writ of error to the Supreme Court, to which the record was remitted. 260 U.S. 703, 43 S. Ct. 163.

The contention here is that the statute, by its terms and as applied in this case, is repugnant to the due process clause of the Fourteenth Amendment. Its material provisions are:

'Sec. 160. Criminal Anarchy Defined. Criminal anarchy is the doctrine that organized government should be overthrown by force or violence, or by assassination [sic] of the executive head or of any of the executive officials of government, or by any unlawful means. The advocacy of such doctrine either by word of mouth or writing is a felony.

'Sec. 161. Advocacy of Criminal Anarchy. Any person who:

'1. By word of mouth or writing advocates, advises or teaches the duty, necessity or propriety of overthrowing or overturning organized government by force or violence, or by assassination of the executive head or of any of the executive officials of government, or by any unlawful means; or,

'2. Prints, publishes, edits, issues or knowingly circulates, sells, distributes or publicly displays any book, paper, document, or written or printed matter in any [268 U.S. 652, 655] form, containing or advocating, advising or teaching the doctrine that organized government should be overthrown by force, violence or any unlawful means, ...

'Is guilty of a felony and punishable' by imprisonment or fine, or both.

The indictment was in two counts. The first charged that the defendant had advocated, advised and taught the duty, necessity and propriety of overthrowing and overturning organized government by force, violence and unlawful means, by certain writings therein set forth entitled 'The Left Wing Manifesto'; the second that he had printed, published and knowingly circulated and distributed a certain paper called 'The Revolutionary Age,' containing the writings set forth in the first count advocating, advising and teaching the doctrine that organized government should be overthrown by force, violence and unlawful means.

The following facts were established on the trial by undisputed evidence and admissions: The defendant is a member of the Left Wing Section of the Socialist Party, a dissenting branch or faction of that party formed in opposition to its dominant policy of 'moderate Socialism.' Membership in both is open to aliens as well as citizens. The Left Wing Section was organized nationally at a conference in New York City in June, 1919, attended by ninety delegates from twenty different States. The conference elected a National Council, of which the defendant was a member, and left to it the adoption of a 'Manifesto.' This was published in The Revolutionary Age, the official organ of the Left Wing. The defendant was on the board of managers of the paper and was its business manager. He arranged for the printing of the paper and took to the printer the manuscript of the first issue which contained the Left Wing Manifesto, and also a Communist Program and a Program of the Left Wing that had been adopted by the conference. Sixteen thousand [268 U.S. 652, 656] copies were printed, which were delivered at the premises in New York City used as the office of the Revolutionary Age and the head quarters of the Left Wing, and occupied by the defendant and other officials. These copies were paid for by the defendant, as business manager of the paper. Employees at this office wrapped and mailed out copies of the paper under the defendant's direction; and copies were sold from this office. It was admitted that the defendant signed a card subscribing to the Manifesto and Program of the Left Wing, which all applicants were required to sign before being admitted to membership; that he went to different parts of the State to speak to branches of the Socialist Party about the principles of the Left Wing and advocated their adoption; and that he was responsible for the Manifesto as it appeared, that 'he knew of the publication, in a general way and he knew of its publication afterwards, and is responsible for the circulation.'

There was no evidence of any effect resulting from the publication and circulation of the Manifesto.

No witnesses were offered in behalf of the defendant.

Extracts from the Manifesto are set forth in the margin. Coupled with a review of the rise of Socialism, it [268 U.S. 652, 657] condemned the dominant 'moderate Socialism' for its recognition of the necessity of the democratic parliamentary state; repudiated its policy of introducing Socialism by legislative measures; and advocated, in plain and unequivocal language, the necessity of accomplishing the 'Communist Revolution' by a militant and 'revolutionary Socialism,' based on 'the class struggle' and mobilizing [268 U.S. 652, 658] the 'power of the proletariat in action,' through mass industrial revolts developing into mass political strikes and 'revolutionary mass action,' for the purpose of conquering and destroying the parliamentary state and establishing in its place, through a 'revolutionary dictatorship of the proletariat,' the system of Communist Socialism. The then recent strikes in Seattle and Winnepeg3 were cited as instances of a development already verging on revolutionary action and suggestive of proletarian [268 U.S. 652, 659] dictatorship, in which the strike-workers were 'trying to usurp the functions of municipal government'; and revolutionary Socialism, it was urged, must use these mass industrial revolts to broaden the strike, make it general and militant, and develop it into mass political strikes and revolutionary mass action for the annihilation of the parliamentary state.

At the outset of the trial the defendant's counsel objected to the introduction of any evidence under the [268 U.S. 652, 660] indictment on the grounds that, as a matter of law, the Manifesto 'is not in contravention of the statute,' and that 'the statute is in contravention of' the due process clause of the Fourteenth Amendment. This objection was denied. They also moved, at the close of the evidence, to dismiss the indictment and direct an acquittal 'on the grounds stated in the first objection to evidence,' [268 U.S. 652, 661] and again on the grounds that 'the indictment does not charge an offense' and the evidence 'does not show an offense.' These motions were also denied.

The court, among other things, charged the jury, in substance, that they must determine what was the intent, purpose and fair meaning of the Manifesto; that its words must be taken in their ordinary meaning, as they would be understood by people whom it might reach; that a mere statement or analysis of social and economic facts and historical incidents, in the nature of an essay, accompanied by prophecy as to the future course of events, but with no teaching, advice or advocacy of action, would not constitute the advocacy, advice or teaching of a doctrine for the overthrow of government within the meaning of the statute; that a mere statement that unlawful acts might accomplish such a purpose would be insufficient, unless there was a teaching, advising the advocacy of employing such unlawful acts for the purpose of overthrowing government; and that if the jury had a reasonable doubt that the Manifesto did teach, advocate or advise the duty, necessity or propriety of using unlawful means for the overthrowing of organized government, the defendant was entitled to an acquittal.

The defendant's counsel submitted two requests to charge which embodied in substance the statement that to constitute criminal anarchy within the meaning of the statute it was necessary that the language used or published should advocate, teach or advise the duty, necessity or propriety of doing 'some definite or immediate act or acts' or force, violence or unlawfulness directed toward the overthrowing of organized government. These were denied further than had been charged. Two other requests to charge embodied in substance the statement that to constitute guilt the language used or published must be 'reasonably and ordinarily calculated to incite certain persons' to acts of force, violence or unlawfulness, [268 U.S. 652, 662] with the object of overthrowing organized government. These were also denied.

The Appellate Division, after setting forth extracts from the Manifesto and referring to the Left Wing and Communist Programs published in the same issue of the Revolutionary Age, said:

> It is perfectly plain that the plan and purpose advocated ... contemplate the overthrow and destruction of the governments of the United States and of all the States, not by the free action of the majority of the people through the ballot box in electing representatives to authorize a change of government by amending or changing the Constitution, ... but by immediately organizing the industrial proletariat into militant Socialist unions and at the earliest opportunity through mass strike and force and violence, if necessary, compelling the government to cease to function, and then through a proletarian dictatorship, taking charge of and appropriating all property and administering it and governing through such dictatorship until such time as the proletariat is permitted to administer and govern it. ... The articles in question are not a discussion of ideas and theories. They advocate a doctrine deliberately determined upon and planned for militantly disseminating a propaganda advocating that it is the duty and necessity of the proletariat engaged in industrial pursuits to organize to such an extent that, by massed strike, the wheels of government may ultimately be stopped and the government overthrown ...

The Court of Appeals held that the Manifesto 'advocated the overthrow of this government by violence, or by unlawful means.' In one of the opinions representing [268 U.S. 652, 663] the views of a majority of the court, it was said:

> It will be seen ... that this defendant through the Manifesto ... advo-
> cated the destruction of the state and the establishment of the dicta-
> torship of the proletariat. ... To advocate ... the commission of this
> conspiracy or action by mass strike whereby government is cripped,
> the administration of justice paralyzed, and the health, morals and
> welfare of a community endangered, and this for the purpose of
> bringing about a revolution in the state, is to advocate the overthrow of
> organized government by unlawful means.

In the other it was said:

> As we read this Manifesto ... we feel entirely clear that the jury were
> justified in rejecting the view that it was a mere academic and harmless
> discussion of the advantages of communism and advanced socialism'
> and 'in regarding it as a justification and advocacy of action by one
> class which would destory the rights of all other classes and overthrow
> the state itself by use of revolutionary mass strikes. It is true that there
> is no advocacy in specific terms of the use of ... force or violence.
> There was no need to be. Some things are so commonly incident to
> others that they do not need to be mentioned when the underlying
> purpose is described.

And both the Appellate Division and the Court of Appeals held the statute constitutional.

The specification of the errors relied on relates solely to the specific rulings of the trial court in the matters hereinbefore set out. The correctness of the verdict is not [268 U.S. 652, 664] questioned, as the case was submitted to the jury. The sole contention here is, essentially, that as there was no evidence of any concrete result flowing from the publication of the Manifesto or of circumstances showing the likelihood of such result, the statute as construed and applied by the trial court penalizes the mere utterance, as such, of 'doctrine' having no quality of incitement, without regard either to the circumstances of its utterance or to the likelihood of unlawful sequences; and that, as the exercise of the right of free expression with relation to government is only punishable 'in circumstances involving likelihood of substantive evil,' the statute contravenes the due process clause of the Fourteenth Amendment. The argument in support of this contention rests primarily upon the following propositions: 1st, That the 'liberty' protected by the Fourteenth Amendment includes the liberty of speech and of the press; and 2d, That while liberty of expression 'is not absolute,' it may be restrained 'only in circumstances where its exercise bears a causal relation with some substantive evil, consummated, attempted or likely,' and as the statute 'takes no account of circumstances,' it unduly restrains this liberty and is therefore unconstitutional.

The precise question presented, and the only question which we can consider under this writ of error, then is, whether the statute, as construed and applied in this case, by the State courts, deprived the defendant of his liberty of expression in violation of the due process clause of the Fourteenth Amendment.

The statute does not penalize the utterance or publication of abstract 'doctrine' or academic discussion having no quality of incitement to any concrete action. It is not aimed against mere historical or philosophical essays. It does not restrain the advocacy of changes in the form of government by constitutional and lawful means. What it prohibits is language advocating, advising or teaching [268 U.S. 652, 665] the overthrow of organized government by unlawful means. These words imply urging to action. Advocacy is defined in the Century Dictionary as: '1. The act of pleading for, supporting, or recommending; active espousal.' It is not the abstract 'doctrine' of overthrowing organized government by unlawful means which is denounced by the statute, but the advocacy of action for the accomplishment of that purpose. It was so construed and applied by the trial judge, who specifically charged the jury that:

> A mere grouping of historical events and a prophetic deduction from them would neither constitute advocacy, advice or teaching of a doctrine for the overthrow of government by force, violence or unlawful means. [And] if it were a mere essay on the subject, as suggested by counsel, based upon deductions from alleged historical events, with no teaching, advice or advocacy of action, it would not constitute a violation of the statute. ...

The Manifesto, plainly, is neither the statement of abstract doctrine nor, as suggested by counsel, mere prediction that industrial disturbances and revolutionary mass strikes will result spontaneously in an inevitable process of evolution in the economic system. It advocates and urges in fervent language mass action which shall progressively foment industrial disturbances and through political mass strikes and revolutionary mass action overthrow and destroy organized parliamentary government. It concludes with a call to action in these words:

> The proletariat revolution and the Communist reconstruction of society—the struggle for these—is now indispensable. ... The Communist International calls the proletariat of the world to the final struggle...

This is not the expression of philosophical abstraction, the mere prediction of future events; it is the language of direct incitement.

The means advocated for bringing about the destruction of organized parliamentary government, namely, mass industrial [268 U.S. 652, 666] revolts usurping the functions of municipal government, political mass strikes directed against the parliamentary state, and revolutionary mass action for its final destruction, necessarily imply the use of force and violence, and in their essential nature are inherently unlawful in a constitutional government of law and order. That the jury were warranted in finding that the Manifesto advocated not merely the abstract doctrine of overthrowing organized government by force, violence and unlawful means, but action to that end, is clear. . .

And, for yet more imperative reasons, a State may punish utterances endangering the foundations of organized government and threatening its overthrow by unlawful means. These imperil its own existence as a constitutional State. Freedom of speech and press, said Story, supra, does not protect disturbances to the public peace or the attempt to subvert the government. It does not protect publications or teachings which tend to subvert or imperil the government or to impede or hinder it in the performance of its governmental duties. State v. [268 U.S. 652, 668] Holm, supra, p. 275 (166 N. W. 181). It does not protect publications prompting the overthrow of government by force; the punishment of those who publish articles which tend to destroy organized society being essential to the security of freedom and the stability of the state. . .

It is clear that the question in such cases is entirely different from that involved in those cases where the statute merely prohibits certain acts involving the danger of substantive evil, without any reference to language itself, and it is sought to apply its provisions to language [268 U.S. 652, 671] used by the defendant for the purpose of bringing about the prohibited results. There, if it be contended that the statute cannot be applied to the language used by the defendant because of its protection by the freedom of speech or press, it must necessarily be found, as an original question, without any previous determination by the legislative body, whether the specific language used involved such likelihood of bringing about the substantive evil as to deprive it of the constitutional protection. In such case it has been held that the general provisions of the statute may be constitutionally applied to the specific utterance of the defendant if its natural tendency and probable effect was to bring about the substantive evil which the legislative body might prevent. Schenck v. United States, supra, p. 51 (39 S. Ct. 247); Debs v. United States, supra, pp. 215, 216 (39 S. Ct. 252). And the general statement in the Schenck Case, p. 52 (39 S. Ct. 249) that the 'question in every case is whether the words used are used in such circumstances and are of such a nature as to create a clear and present danger that they will bring about the substantive evils,'—upon which great reliance is placed in the defendant's argument—was manifestly intended, as shown by the context, to apply only in cases of this class, and has no application to those like the present, where the legislative body itself has previously determined the danger of substantive evil arising from utterances of a specified character.

The defendant's brief does not separately discuss any of the rulings of the trial court. It is only necessary to say that, applying the general rules already stated, we find that none of them involved any invasion of the constitutional rights of the defendant. It was not necessary, within the meaning of the statute, that the defendant should have advocated 'some definite or immediate act or acts' of force, violence or unlawfulness. It was sufficient if such acts were advocated in general terms; and it was not essential that their immediate execution should [268 U.S. 652, 672] have been advocated. Nor was it necessary that the language should have been 'reasonably and ordinarily calculated to incite certain persons' to acts of force, violence or unlawfulness. The advocacy need not be addressed to specific persons. Thus, the publication and circulation of a newspaper article may be an encouragement or endeavor to persuade to murder, although not addressed to any person in particular. Queen v. Most, L. R. 7 Q. B. D. 244.

We need not enter upon a consideration of the English common law rule of seditious libel or the Federal Sedition Act of 1798, to which reference is made in the defendant's brief. These are so unlike the present statute, that we think the decisions under them cast no helpful light upon the questions here.

And finding, for the reasons stated, that the statute is not in itself unconstitutional, and that it has not been applied in the present case in derogation of any constitutional right, the judgment of the Court of Appeals is

AFFIRMED.

Source: *Gitlow v. People of State of New York* (268 U.S. 652, 1925).

Index